C000161844

How
First-Class
Business Essays
and Dissertations

ISBN 978-0-9929202-8-9

Copyright © 2016 by Vlad Mackevic

How to Write First-Class Business Essays and Dissertations

Vlad Mackevic

Published by Hallow Books in association with

www.TheLectureRoom.co.uk

Copyright © 2016 by Vlad Mackevic.

PUBLISHED BY: Hallow Books and Mackevic, Birmingham, United Kingdom

Book Cover Design © Vlad Mackevic. Image **12480344** by **Yellowj** from Bigstock (Royalty Free Images)

All rights reserved. Without limiting the rights under copyright reserved above, no part of this publication may be reproduced, stored in or introduced into a retrieval system, or transmitted, in any form, or by any means (electronic, mechanical, photocopying, recording, or otherwise) without the prior written permission of both the copyright owners and the above publisher of this book.

The information this book contains is based on the author's personal experience. Please do not assume and hereby disclaim any liability to any party for any loss, damage, or disruption caused by possible differences between the author's experience and that of his readers. Although the author and publisher have made every effort to ensure that the information in this book was correct at press time, the author and publisher do not assume and hereby disclaim any liability to any party for any loss, damage, or disruption caused by errors or omissions, whether such errors or omissions result from negligence, accident, or any other cause. All websites and brand names are used in this book for information purposes only, and the author is in no way endorsing them or promoting them for any purpose.

CONTENTS

A Very Short Introduction

Thank you for picking up this book!

I assume that you are (or are going to be) a university student. Most probably, you are or will be studying a degree subject related to Business, Management, HR, Economics, Finance or Marketing. And you are reading this book because you have to write an academic assignment.

It doesn't even matter what kind of assignment it is – a first year essay or a Master's dissertation. What matters is that you want to become better at what you're doing – and I want to help you. In this book, I promise to share all I know about essay, exam and dissertation writing.

So, why should you read my book and not any other?

I could list several reasons. Maybe it is because I have a first-class degree myself. Perhaps it is because I turned three of my undergraduate essays into journal publications, so I should know what I'm talking about, right? Maybe it's because I have taught academic writing, study skills, and English for Business and Engineering for more than six years. I've also worked in marketing, where I had to learn another writing style – that of business professionals.

All of these reasons look good enough, don't they? However, the main reason is the fact that, just like you, I've been a student. I was a frightened first year who did not know anything about academic writing. I was a confident second year who thought he knew everything (it was not the case, as I learnt later). I was also a doubtful final year student who was very critical about the results of his own research as well as that of others.

In other words, I've *been there and done that*. I have quite a lot of experience, as a teacher and as a learner. And I know exactly how you feel. I want to help you become the best you can, help you achieve success.

I have a lot of writing experience, both at university and outside of it. And I want to share it with you.

As a writer, I know that writing is hard work. I know that academic writing is even harder. When you come to university, no one explains anything to you – certainly not your lecturers. You need to seek help in libraries and academic writing centres (luckily, these now exist in every university). Yet, you can only see someone in those centres for an hour at most, once a week.

That's why I'm writing this book: I want to help you become a successful student. I know how university assignments work; moreover, I know how to *make them work.*

I'm writing this book to make it easier for you to score 10-30% higher in *every* assignment you submit. Yes, I mean it! Because it's nothing but pure technique. The key is to become aware of what you are doing: how you are writing your assignments, what exactly you are doing well and whether there are any areas that need improvement. Once you start consciously applying the methods I outline in this book, you will boost your grades and be a first-class student before you know it.

Let's get started and good luck on your academic journey!

Chapter 1

Academic Writing

We will start with the basics. At the start of this chapter, I will explain the differences between learning and teaching at school and at university. Next, I will tell you what a good essay should contain and what you get marks for in the marking system. One of the greatest problems that students face at university is the lack of information; every module has a document called 'Marking Criteria', which should tell you what matters when writing an essay. However, not that many students know where to find it and even fewer actually read it. The reason is quite simple: marking criteria documents are usually quite boring and a bit difficult to understand. I will try to make it clear for you in this chapter.

1.1. School vs. University

There are quite a few differences between the way learning and teaching takes place at school or sixth form/college and university. Let me explain them:

a. The role of the teacher

At school, the teacher is always present to explain something if the students do not understand. The teacher is the facilitator of learning; their only job is to make sure that learning takes place. At university, on the other hand, lecturers are not facilitators of learning. Most of the time, they are only delivering information. Of course, some classes are seminars and workshops where learning is more interactive. However, lecturers have many more responsibilities than just teaching: they need to do research and publish articles; they need to do a lot of administrative work, too. If they are also heads of departments, they need to work as managers as well. Therefore, they don't have that much time for the students. It's hard to see them even during office hours – especially in business schools because the business school is the largest one in almost every university and the office hours tend to be overbooked all the time. The teacher is not there to guide you – you need to learn a lot independently.

b. Learning style

Let's face it – at school, the students are spoon-fed information. It is broken down into small, manageable chunks and the students are told what they should know. University is different. If you are already studying at university, you will know that if you have six modules per term, every module has around 100 hours assigned to it. Out of these, 20-22 hours are actual classes (lectures and seminars). The rest is mostly independent study – either individually or in groups. This involves a lot of reading: reading to prepare for seminars, reading that has been assigned as homework, reading in preparation for your exams and essays, etc. You need to be disciplined in order to work on your own, without anyone breathing down your neck.

c. Rules of writing

At school, there are not that many rules concerning essay writing. A lot of emphasis is placed on creativity, on not restricting the students' freedom. When it comes to university, the students are expected to obey all sorts of rules. First of all, your writing must be formal; secondly, you must reference your sources, which means that you need to tell your reader where your information comes from (sadly, no one explains how to do that and you must learnt it by yourself); thirdly, you have to be less descriptive and more critical (nobody explains what that means, either); fourthly, you are not really allowed to say 'I think' or 'in my opinion' – you must find out what *others* think and present *their* opinions; moreover, you cannot copy anything word-for-word like at school. You must learn to rewrite other people's ideas in your own words (it's called *summarising* and *paraphrasing*). These rules, especially in your first year, can make you feel like you are not allowed to be creative or original.

d. Your information sources

At school, nobody *really* cares where you got your information from. As long as you can present it nicely and write with conviction, you can get good grades. At university, in order to be considered seriously, you should carefully select your information sources. Books published by serious academic publishers (e.g. Palgrave, Routledge or different University Presses) are good; so are academic journal articles, professional media articles and websites of organisations. However, if the information you are using comes from Wikipedia, a gossipy tabloid newspaper or a website that cannot be linked to a respectable business or government organisation (for example, a private blog), then it may not be a good idea to use such sources. You need to check your information carefully.

As I mentioned before, universities emphasise independent learning. Every lecturer thinks that their subject is the most important one and that you should dedicate all your time to learning for the exam or preparing an essay in that particular subject. Managing your time well is vital, too.

1.2. What Do You Get Points For?

Before you start your essay, it's a good idea to find out what your lecturers are looking for. As I mentioned earlier, every module has a set of marking criteria. Let me simplify these and present them to you.

At university, you get marks for the following elements of your assignment:

- Answering the question
- Structure and organisation
- Style and language
- Research and references
- Analysis, understanding and interpretation
- Formatting and presentation

These elements are not listed in any order of importance. They are all equally important and every single one of them will earn you points – which all add up and amount to higher grades. I will briefly explain each element.

a. Answering the question

Despite the fact that this sounds obvious, everything you write in your assignment must be done with a sole purpose – answering the question. This is especially difficult when you can choose your topic yourself because you need to create an essay question that is *easy to answer* (I will talk more about it in **Chapter 2**).

Answering the question means that everything in your essay should be about one topic. For example, let's imagine that your essay question is *Discuss the advantages and disadvantages of Social Media Marketing.* You've read a lot of different books and articles about it and one particular book explains how marketing on Facebook, Twitter, Youtube, Pinterest and Instagram is very different from the older forms of marketing, like in print media or over the phone. The book describes different systems of marketing in a lot of detail, including their history and how they developed and changed over time. It is very important to remember that you are NOT writing a book and you have no time or space in your essay to talk about any of this. In fact, you might not even have the space to talk about all the social media the book mentions, and you will need to choose one or two. Your word count (2000-4000 words, depending on your year of study) will only allow you to introduce social media marketing very briefly and talk about its benefits and drawbacks using real-life examples that you take from academic articles. You do not need to write about history or compare modern marketing to traditional marketing. Everything you write must be closely related to the topic of your essay.

b. Structure and organisation

The structure is the 'formula' according to which you write your essay, research report or dissertation. It is a special way of organising your writing to make it flow coherently from the beginning to the end. The most basic structure of any academic assignment is *Introduction – Main Body – Conclusion.* The paragraphs also have a structure of their own. I cover this in more depth in **Chapter 3.**

The majority of the chapters in this book deal with the 'building blocks' of academic work – the introduction, previous research, methodology, analysis, discussion and the conclusion. In subsequent chapters, I will describe each of these, telling you what they consist of and how they should be written to make your academic writing more effective.

c. Style and language

At university you are expected to write your assignments in formal English. To do this, you will need to know the difference between spoken and written language, how to write in an appropriate academic style and avoid basic mistakes that make your writing look unprofessional. You will also need to learn to think and write like an academic.

This, however, does not mean you need to use big words and long, complicated sentences all the time. Your writing can be plain and simple, and yet very impressive. See **Chapter 13: The Language of Academia** and **Chapter 14: Writing Tips** for more information.

d. Research and references

There are several questions that you should think about when you are doing research. Here they are:

- Is my research **relevant**? Is what I am reading helping me answer my question?
- Is my research **broad enough**? Have I read enough about my topic?

- Is my research **deep enough**? Do I know the theories that can help me answer my question? Do I know how those theories were applied and tested in real life? Useful tip: theory is found in textbooks; real life applications can be found in academic journal articles.

- Is my research **reliable enough**? Am I using reputable sources of information? Who is the creator of the website I am using? Who is the author of the article I am quoting?

Referencing (telling your reader where you got your information from) is one of the most difficult parts of your essay. It is difficult because when you compile your list of references, you need to include a lot of information about each book (the author, the date of publication, the title of the book, article or journal, the page numbers, the place of publication and the publishing house; if the resource is electronic, usually you also need to include the web link and the date when you accessed it). The basic principle of referencing is as follows:

If you write about an idea that is not yours but was taken from someone else's book or article, you have to give credit to that person and write their name next to the idea. The same applies to any figures and statistics: you need to tell your reader where you got them from, otherwise it looks like you've made them up.

Referencing is all about respecting the work of others, not stealing someone else's thoughts and – most importantly – informing your readers that your information comes from reliable sources. You can find more information on referencing in **Chapter 10: Referencing**.

e. Analysis, understanding and interpretation

These elements of your essay show how well you are able to understand what you've read and to engage with the material. You need to be able to show you reader that:

- You are able to read a complicated document and then report on its contents and in your own words.

- You are able to read several complicated documents and compare the information in them. You are able to summarise many documents based on these comparisons.

- You are able to write critically. This means that you do not believe the first author you read – rather, you compare what several people have written and see how similar or different their views are.

- You are able to select the right sources for your essay – books, academic journal articles, conference papers, reputable newspapers, and trustworthy websites.

- You are able to compare your own results with the results of other researchers. You are able to say how similar or different your results are from those of other studies and why they are similar or different.

- You are able to make links between theory and practice. The theory comes from textbooks. The practical examples come from academic journal articles that describe how the theory was tested and applied in the real world.

I would like to talk about *being critical* a little more. It is important to read different authors and examine their views on the subject. Are they similar or different? Moreover, how similar are their data and research methods to those you used? How similar or different are their results to your results? It also means acknowledging the limitations of *your* research. The theory you are using is not the only one available and all theories have limitations. Your data and your results will always present a limited picture; your method is not the only correct one either! For a more in-depth discussion on this topic, see **Chapter 8: Analysis and Discussion.**

f. Formatting and Presentation

If you invited your guests to dinner, you wouldn't serve them food on dirty plates.

The same applies to your essay. As your lecturer reads your work, sloppy formatting can be as insulting as a coffee stain across the page. Moreover, formatting usually constitutes five per cent of your mark, so a well-formatted and professionally presented essay can make a difference between a 2:1 and a first!

Make fonts uniform, leave wide margins, double-space your lines and add a conservative cover page – all of this is important. Read more about it in **Chapter 15: Formatting and Presentation.**

1.3. Different Genres of Academic Writing

There are many different types, or genres, of academic writing in the business schools of the universities around the world. Every student should know how to write these types of essays. Here are the main genres (this list has been adapted from *www.UEfAP.com/writing*):

a. Essay

The essay is the most popular genre of academic writing. Essays can be very short (1,000 words) and quite long (4,000-5,000 words). You would normally write shorter essays in your first year of university and longer ones during your final year and your Master's degree.

The basic principle of any essay is *the argument*. Arguing simply means providing a view or an opinion on a topic and then providing evidence which supports that opinion. The evidence should come from the literature you have read. Please note that en essay will often have two arguments. In other words, there will be *two different points of view*, and you will have to find evidence to support both of them.

Although you are not supposed to use the words *I think* and *in my opinion* in your academic essays, you can still express your ideas. However, you also need to find published works in which similar ideas are expressed and reference them.

The argument of the essay can be based around comparing and contrasting, explaining, discussing whether something is true or not, important or not, valuable or not, providing and analysing the reasons and consequences of something, discussing the advantages and disadvantages, etc.

The academic essay should be structured in this way:

Front Matter	Title page (every university has different requirements)
Main Text	1. Introduction (background to the study, the research question, the object, the context and the method of the study). I will explain it more

	detail in **Chapter 2**.
	2. Main Body
	2.1. First point of view
	a. First idea
	b. Second idea
	c. …
	2.2. Second (often opposite) point of view
	a. First idea
	b. Second idea
	c. …
	3. Conclusion (a brief summary of the main body)
Back Matter	1. References (the list of books, journals and websites that you used in your research)
	2. Any appendices

b. Report

Academic reports are another genre of academic writing that business students should be familiar with. Reports are detailed accounts of a study or an experiment. You tell your reader what you wanted to research, how you did it (in as much detail as possible), how the experiment went, what the results were and why you think the results were like this and not different. You also compare your results to those of other researchers and say how similar and different they are. The purpose of the study is not just to answer any essay question. Rather, the purpose is to:

a. Read the existing literature on the topic of your study.

b. Identify an area you would like to explore deeper. It could be an experiment that someone else has done before and you would like to repeat it to see if you get the same results with different data (for example, involving different people in your study or analysing a different organisation). It could also be an under-researched area (a knowledge gap) and you would like to start filling this gap.

The report is structured in the following way:

Front Matter	Title page (every university has different requirements)
	Abstract (a short summary of the report)
	Contents (because the report is usually long and is made of many sections, so your reader needs to find each section easily).
Main Text	1. Introduction and research background. Sometimes the research background can be a different section. In this case, you describe what other people did before you and how you would like to add to their findings. You should always include the research question.
	2. Methodology (talk about your data and about your research methods)
	3. Findings/Results
	4. Discussion (why, in your opinion, the results were like they were; how your results are similar or different from those of other researchers, etc.)
	5. Conclusion

Back Matter	1. References
	2. Any appendices

Let's take an example of a typical report. Let's imagine that you know that company X, which specialises in selling office equipment, has become a very successful business. You want to find out what may have led to this success. There has been no change in management, no employees were hired or dismissed, so you suspect that the reason for the company's success must be the marketing. However, you are not sure yet.

Your report will be called *An analysis of the effects of marketing on the financial success of Company X*.

You will begin by writing a few sentences about Company X and about their recent financial success. You can also show the sales figures for the last couple of years in graphs and compare them. Then you will introduce your research question: what are the reasons for the financial success of Company X? You will also have a hypothesis – a research statement that you need to either prove or disprove. Your hypothesis will be *Marketing has been important for the financial success of Company X*. Your literature review will talk about other people's research on the effect of marketing on business performance.

Next, you will talk about the research methods. In order to find out the reasons, you decide to contact the organisation and interview their employees. You also design a questionnaire and send it to the organisation so that it can be distributed among the employees. This approach, when you do the research yourself, is called *primary research*.

While you are waiting for the answer from Company X, you decide to examine what the newspapers, magazines and academic journals have been writing about the company in order to get some background information. Analysing the research of other people to support your research is called *secondary research*. This secondary research might also go into your literature review section.

Company X writes back to you. Thirty people have filled in your questionnaire and you understand from their answers that the reason for the increase in sales is the marketing. Moreover, two employees from the sales and marketing department have agreed to speak to you about it. During the interview they tell you that they decided to improve their customer experience by including very detailed descriptions of their products on their website and by uploading photos, and sometimes also videos with reviews, of every product so that their customers would be able to see what they were buying.

You write several paragraphs about your research methods (this is you *Methodology* section) as well as about the results of your research (this is your **analysis)**. Next, you start looking for articles about the importance of visual marketing and the use of images and detailed information in promotional literature and online. You select the most relevant articles, include them in your literature review and write about the links between previous research on this topic and what you've found out. This becomes your *Discussion* section.

In the end, you write your conclusion where you summarise your research results.

c. Reflective writing

Reflective writing often causes confusion because it is very different from other forms of academic writing. While the language of your essays, reports and dissertations must be formal and impersonal, the rules of reflective writing allow the use of the pronouns *I* and *we*. You write about your personal experiences and your account is much more personal. However, this does not mean that you should forget about other rules of academic writing. Even if you are writing from a personal point of view, you should still use references and link your experiences to the existing theory and academic research. Your writing must also be formal.

A good example of a title for a reflective essay would be *Choose two motivation theories and describe how they can be applied to your studies and/or work experience.* When writing such an essay, you would reflect on your personal experience using academic theories from books and previous research from journal articles.

When writing a reflective piece, you might be asked to reflect on:

- How to choose a subject for your dissertation;
- How to approach your dissertation;
- How well you wrote a piece of work;
- How you prepared for a lecture;
- How you listened to a lecture;
- How you undertook a reading assignment;
- How you performed in a recent examination;
- How you contributed to some group work;
- How others reacted;
- What you did in a practical situation;
- What experiences you gained in some part-time or voluntary work you did;

- How what you learnt in lectures can be applied to real life;
- How you solved a particular problem;
- How you can improve your research study;

In your reflection, you could write about:

- What you did and why you did it;
- What was good and bad about it;
- Why you found it good or bad;
- What you found easy or difficult;
- Why you found it easy or difficult;
- What you liked about what you did;
- Why you felt like that;
- How you might want to follow it up;
- What other people did and why they did it;
- How you felt about what others did;
- How you used what you have been taught in class;
- What other information you need;
- What you are going to do differently in this type of situation next time;
- What steps you are going to take on the basis of what you have learned;
- What you are going to do next;

Reflective writing often involves an action plan in which you should write about:

- What you are going to do differently in this type of situation next time;

- What steps you are going to take on the basis of what you have learned;

(The questions have been taken from *www.UEfAP.com/writing*)

As you can see from the questions, it is important to describe not only what happened but also why you think it happened. This is part of your critical reflection.

d. Dissertation

A dissertation (either for your undergraduate degree or your Master's degree) is an extended piece of work (usually 10,000-15,000 word long). Your dissertation should be structured similarly to a report (see the table below). Please note, however, that dissertations are different and not all of them will have all the elements from the table.

Front Matter	Title page (every university has different requirements)
	Abstract (a brief summary of your dissertation)
	Table of Contents (to help your reader find his/her way in the long document).
	List of tables and/or figures
Main Text	1. Introduction (and research background)
	2. Literature review (previous research on the topic, background for your study, theories and their applications in real life)
	3. Aims of the dissertation (research goals and/or research questions)

	4. Methodology (talk about your data and about your research methods/research design)
	5. Findings/Results
	6. Discussion (why, in your opinion, the results were like they were; how your results are similar or different from those of other researchers, etc.)
	7. Limitations (because no dataset is perfect and no set of findings is universal)
	8. Recommendations for further research (because your research answered the question only in a limited way)
	9. Conclusion and implications of your research. What do your results mean for the real world? Can you make recommendations for business professionals based on your research?
Back Matter	1. References (a list of literature you used for your research)
	2. Any appendices

If any of these elements are confusing, do not worry – I will explain more about each of them later in this book.

Now, once I've explained the most widespread genres of academic writing, let's move on to the first element of any academic piece: the title. **Chapter 2** explains how to understand and create an essay title.

FURTHER READING

Hounsell, D. (1995). Marking and Commenting on Essays. *Tutoring and Demonstrating: a Handbook.* Edinburgh: Centre for Teaching, Learning and Assessment, The University of Edinburgh. Chapter 6. [Online]. Available at: http://bit.ly/1di0Z6b (Accessed May 2016).

Redman, P. (2006). What Tutors Look For When Marking Essays. *Good Essay Writing,* Third edition. London: Sage Publications. Chapter 2. [Online]. Available at http://bit.ly/1dShLFT (Accessed May 2016).

Leeds University Business School (2016) School Assessment Criteria/Marking Scheme – Undergraduate. *Leeds University*

Business School [Online]. Available at: http://bit.ly/1TuqEtv (Accessed May 2016)

The University of Exeter (2014).Marking criteria for essays and presentations. *The University of Exeter* [Online]. Available at: http://bit.ly/1fCOUFc (Accessed February 2014).

UEFAP (2014). Genres in Academic Writing. *UEfAP* [Online]. Available at: http://www.uefap.com/writing/ (Accessed January 2014).

Chapter 2

How to Understand (and Create) an Essay Question

If I were to put essay questions into any groups or categories, there would be only two: those given to you by your lecturer and those created by you. In this chapter, I will explain how to understand what your lecturer wants you to write about (it's not as easy as it seems because sometimes essay questions can be rather complicated) and how to create an essay question that is easy to answer if you can choose a topic for your essay yourself.

2.1. Analysing the Essay Question (Set Questions)

An academic essay is usually a written assignment with a **given (pre-set) topic**. You already know what the topic is – you just need to understand it through breaking it down into its component parts, and answer it.

An essay question is usually made of three parts: the *object* of the study, the *context* of the study and the *method* of the study. Let me explain these in more detail.

The object of the study

The *object* is the main topic of the essay. It is usually a noun or a noun phrase. For example, if the essay title is *What are the advantages and disadvantages of Facebook marketing?* the object of the study will be Facebook Marketing. The object of the study also limits the scope of the research you have to carry out: you only need to look for books and articles on Facebook marketing and not on any other types of marketing.

The context of the study

The *context* means *circumstances*. When we talk about the context of anything, we ask the questions *When?* and *Where?* Often the context is not only physical but also theoretical: the essay can look at phenomena and events using a certain theory. For example, if the essay title is **Discuss if Abraham Maslow's Hierarchy of Needs theory is still applicable in organisations in the 21st century**, the context will be the actual Maslow's theory *and* the 21st century. You will need to learn about the theory, how it was applied in the past, what other people have found out when testing and applying it, and then look at the context of the 21st century and see if it can be applied now. Once again, knowing the context makes your research work easier: after learning about the theory from text books, you will only need to look for articles that talk about Maslow's theory and were published after the year 2000.

The method of the study

If the object of the study is the *What?* and the context is the *When?* and *Where?*, the method is the *How?* of your essay. Let us take the previous examples. In the essay about Facebook marketing, the method words will be *advantages and disadvantages*. We all know what these words mean and it is not difficult to write an essay that answers this question. However, when it comes to the essay question about Maslow's theory, the

24

method word (*discuss*) is a little more complicated. To discuss means to give two different opinions. Usually, these opinions are that:

1. Something _is_ the case because:
   - Reason A
   - Reason B
   - Reason C

2. On the other hand, it _is not_ the case because:
   - Reason A
   - Reason B
   - Reason C

Therefore, the discussion will have two arguments: that Maslow's theory can be applied in the 21st century and that it cannot. Let me explain the object, the context and the method in more detail, using the following examples:

Example 1

Modern organisations often replace the traditional hierarchical structure with a more 'horizontal' team structure. Select two motivation theories from the field of organisational psychology and explain how they can be applied in a team-based organisation.

This essay question seems really complicated – primarily because the title is long and confusing. To make it less complicated, you can break it down into separate components and *extract* the object, the context and the method of the study from the title. Let's begin!

The object of the study

The object of the study in this essay topic is the 'horizontal' tem structure. This is what you should research and find the definition for.

The context of the study

As mentioned before, the context means *circumstances*. The *When?* and the *Where?* are not stated. Rather, they are implicit. The *When?* is *now*. The answer to the question *Where?* is *in team-based organisations*. You are also given a theoretical context – *select two motivation theories*. It is interesting that you need to set the theoretical context yourself.

NB: When you have the freedom to select the theories by yourself, it is a good idea to search for academic articles about these theories to see which ones are mentioned more often. If you choose to write about something that is widely discussed, it will make it easier for you to do your research.

The method of the study

The method of the study is expressed by the verb *explain*. This word is rather simple and your essay should be more descriptive. Yet, when you describe how these theories that you have selected can be applied to team-based organisations, you need to provide examples from literature. This means that you writing will still be critical because you are comparing what different authors say and making links between theory and practice. Moreover, when you provide these examples, it is logical to assume that you select the most relevant ones from the literature you read. Therefore, you are critical even in your choice of examples.

Example 2

What were the reasons for the economic miracle of South Korea in the second half of the twentieth century?

This essay question is pretty straightforward. However, it is worth keeping in mind that even questions like this involve something more than just listing the reasons you have found in the literature. Your lecturers normally expect you to either *present two opposing points of view* or *group your arguments according to certain criteria.*

So, let's start by finding the three elements:

The object of the study

Quite obviously, it is South Korea's economic development.

The context of the study

The context is the time-frame: the second half of the twentieth century. Therefore, you do not need to analyse what happened before this time (unless it led to vital changes in the second half of the twentieth century). Focus on events within the essay time-frame. Don't wander too far away from the essay question. Of course, your essay will be relatively short. For this reason, you will not be able to write about every event that happened between the years 1950 and 2000. It is a good idea to select several key events in that period and write about them.

The method of the study

The method is not expressed as a verb this time. Rather, it is a noun – *reasons.* You need to *find the reasons* – but not just list them in any random order. In an ideal situation, your reasons should be grouped under two slightly opposing categories.

You can usually divide the reasons behind any change into two types: internal and external. It doesn't matter if the change happens at an individual level, the level of an organisation or at a national level.

For example, factors that influence an individual's motivation can be grouped into internal (personality, personal goals and aspirations) and external (the influence of the team, of the leader, or of the organisation's policies).

The reasons for the success of a team or a company can be internal (good management, clear roles, sense of a common goal) and external (lack of competition, good economic conditions, a market gap). The same applies to failure. The reasons for failure can be internal (bad leadership, role ambiguity when team members are not sure exactly what their job is, stress, motivation) or external (a competitor uses certain strategies that the company does not use, lack of financial resources, unfavourable economic conditions, etc.)

I am not claiming that this rule is universal, but dividing arguments into two groups, the first one involving internal processes in a social group, an organisation, or even a country, and the second one related to the external context, is a good start for many assignments that ask you to list reasons.

2.2. Different Method Words and What They Mean

There are many method words (more commonly known as known action words) that can be found in essay titles. The majority of these are very clear. I will list a few words in this section that are commonly used and can sometimes create confusion.

Analyse

When you are asked to analyse something, you are asked to provide a detailed comparison of the causes and any possible effects on the object of your study. The word *analyse* means 'study in detail'.

A good example of an essay title containing this word is *Analyse the extent to which foreign aid promotes economic development.* This means that you need to say how much positive influence foreign aid has on the economic development of the countries that receive it. Wherever it is possible, try to provide examples; it is very important to provide evidence from literature to support your arguments. You need to study the effects of foreign aid in detail.

Assess

If you are asked to assess something, you need to measure and judge the magnitude or quality of something. In other words, you need to analyse something and say how big/important/good something is.

The most important part of an essay that assesses something is the reasoning: providing reasons why something is important or unimportant. A good example of an essay with this word is: *Assess the economic implications of the movement of many Eastern and Central European countries from planned economies to market economies.* When answering this essay question, you need to say whether moving from planned to market economies was good/important for these countries' economies or not and provide evidence to support your view.

Compare/Compare and Contrast

This question word is quite simple. It asks you to describe two situations and present the similarities and differences between them. A description of the two situations does not on its own meet the requirements of this key term. You need to be very explicit and point out the similarities and the differences. An example of an essay question with this word is *Compare the effectiveness of demand-side economic policies to supply-side policies in reducing the level of unemployment.*

Evaluate

This has the word 'value' hidden in it. When you are asked to evaluate something, you need to tell your readers how 'valuable' or big or important something is. Is it very important? Is it not important at all? An example of an essay question containing this word would be *Evaluate the role of the Internet in Human Resource Management, especially with regard to personnel recruitment.*

In this essay, you will need to discuss how important or unimportant the Internet is for the process of recruiting new staff in organisations. In fact, this method word is somewhat similar to the word *assess* above.

- When factors such as causes, consequences or remedies are asked for, students should attempt to identify the most important ones and then to justify the reason for the choice.

- When advantages and disadvantages are asked for, students should attempt to identify the most important advantage (or disadvantage) and then justify the reason for the choice.

- When strategies are asked for, students should attempt to assess the short term and long term implications.

- When data is offered, students may question its validity, in terms of whether it is appropriate, whether it is reliable, or whether it is still relevant.

- When summarising a theory, students may also question its validity, in terms of whether it is appropriate, whether it is reliable, or whether it is still relevant.

- A stakeholder analysis can also be used as a way of evaluating the effects of an economic policy/decision.

Source: http://www.itseducation.asia/dictionary/essay.htm

Outline

Outlining is really simple. It means just describing or explaining the main features of something. It can also mean briefly explaining why something is or is not happening. For example, an essay question containing the word *outline* can be *Choose and outline two leadership theories; discuss how those theories can be applied in the workplace using examples from literature as well as from your own work experience.*

2.3. Creating Essay and Dissertation Questions

The title of your essay is probably the most important part. Particularly if you have to create one yourself. When you have a free choice of topic for your university essay, research paper or dissertation, you can have mixed feelings about it. On the one hand, you are excited, because you can write about whatever you want. On the other – you can be overwhelmed: 'How do I figure out what to write about?'

31

One of the most important things you need to think about when creating an essay question is making sure that it is easy to answer. Don't make it hard for yourself, it's not worth it.

So, how do you create a question that is easy to answer? Generally there are three main rules which you have to follow:

1. Choose a narrow, focused topic
2. Pick a subject you love
3. Write about what you know

Let's look at them, one by one.

2.3.1. Choose a Narrow, Focused Topic

Your assignment should not be about a thousand things. It should be about *one*. So, make sure your topic is focused. Let's take this example:

The rise of the Asian Tigers (economic power in the East)

When your readers see this topic, they may ask: 'What on earth are the Asian Tigers?' And even if they know that your essay is about the four powerful economic regions of Asia (Hong Kong, Singapore, South Korea and Taiwan), they may ask the following questions: 'What about them? Which aspect of that phenomenon are you analysing? What were the reasons for their emergence? What were the consequences? Or perhaps you want to carry out an analysis of their economic performance in the past decade?'

You cannot write everything you know about South East Asian economics. You have to narrow your topic down as much as possible.

So, how can you narrow this one down? Let's look at this example:

What were the reasons for the rise of the South Korean high-tech industry in the 1950s?

Here, we are talking about reasons and *not* consequences; South Korea and *not* Taiwan, Hong Kong or Singapore; high-tech and *not* fishing or coal and steel, and the 1950s and *not* any other time. You can even narrow that time down to a period of 20 years.

Can you see? This is narrow. This is focused. This is specific.

Why is this good?

Because it helps two people: you and your reader. For you, it reduces the amount of work. When you have specified in your topic what you are looking for, you have to find books, journals and other publications only about that topic and nothing else! This makes your library search as well as Google search more specific. It is easy to search for specific keywords because they give you a sense of direction. Moreover, if your topic is narrow, you help your readers. When they read your paper, they have a clear idea what they are going to read about.

In short, create a simple, focused question – and then answer it.

2.3.2. Pick a Subject You Love

This is simple and straightforward: if you love something, you will be enthusiastic about it. If you love your subject, you will happily research and write about it.

Writing about a subject simply because it is fashionable or in the news will not make you motivated. If you do not love what you're writing about, it might even make you hate writing your assignment and produce sloppy work. Writing about what you love, on the other hand, will give you ideas and make you want to find out more.

There are no bad essay topics. Especially when you have the freedom to create your own. As long as your essay answers your question, you will get marks.

2.3.3. Write about Something You Know

If you love your topic, you will be keen to learn about it. However, if you are not very enthusiastic about an essay and simply have a duty to do it – then write about something you know.

Learning from scratch is hard. Trust me, I know. Unless you *love* the subject.

So, if you have at least some rudimentary knowledge of an area, write about it. You can even use your previous notes or some old references, which will make things much easier. However, it is important to note that you should not re-use your old essays. You cannot just copy and paste sections of your old work into a new assignment. This is called self-plagiarism and is an academic offence. If you are using your old essays, you can use the ideas, but you will have to rewrite them in different words (paraphrase).

FURTHER READING

Kinmond, K. (2012). 'Coming up with a research question'. In Sullivan, C., Gibson, S. and Riley, S. C. E. (eds.) *Doing Your Qualitative Psychology Project*. London: Sage Publications, Chapter 2, pp. 23-35 [Online]. Available at: http://bit.ly/1ncfb7J (Accessed April 2016)

Sage Publications (no date). 'How can I create a good research hypothesis?' *Sage Publications* [Online]. Available at: http://bit.ly/1j5GojX (Accessed April 2016)

Torres-Reyna, O. (no date). 'Finding data (w/comments on crafting research questions).' *Princeton University* [Online]. Available at: http://bit.ly/1lD7dxu (Accessed April 2016)

The University of Birmingham (no date).'Formulating the Research Question'. *The University of Birmingham* [Online]. Available at: http:///1jADhGA (Accessed April 2016)

Chapter 3

The Structure of an Academic Assignment

The first thing you need to know about essays and dissertations is that they have a certain structure. There is a formula, a particular order in which academic works are written. There are also formulas for writing the entire separate paragraphs. I will explain more about all of these in this chapter.

3.1. The Beginning, the Middle, and the End

Absolutely any essay, research report or dissertation follows a very simple structure or formula. Roughly speaking, the formula looks like this:

1. The Introduction (10-15% of the word count)
2. The Main Body (70-80% of the word count)
3. The Conclusion (10-15% of the word count)

In other words, the essay structure could also be described like this:

1. Say what you're going to say (give your reader an overview of the topic of your essay).
2. Say it (develop the topic in several paragraphs).
3. Say what you've just said (summarise your main body, restating the main ideas).

These three elements are rudimentary, but they are composed of many other, more complex elements. All of these will be analysed in depth later in this book.

3.2. How to Write a Paragraph

Essays are made of paragraphs. Just like when writing an essay, paragraph writing also has some rules. These rules are very simple:

1. Usually one paragraph contains one idea. For example, if you analyse the advantages and disadvantages of something, each advantage or disadvantage will occupy one paragraph.

2. Each paragraph should be connected to the next one. The ideas should flow from one another. You can make them flow by using connecting words

Your paragraphs should be structured to include:

a. A topic sentence

b. An explanation of the topic sentence

c. A piece of evidence that supports the topic sentence. Here you can do the following:

- Give examples to illustrate your idea.
- Provide a quotation or reference that supports your topic statement.
- Anticipate counterarguments and respond to them.
- Offer another perspective to the idea (to provide a balanced opinion).

d. An explanation of the significance of that evidence (why it is important or relevant)

e. A concluding sentence **(optional)**

Please see an example of a paragraph structured in this way below. The numbers mark the following elements:

(1) The introductory sentence

(2) A reference and a quote that elaborates the argument

(3) Logical conclusion from what the referenced author says, explaining why what is said above is relevant

(4) Coming back to today's context; linking to the essay question

(5) Responding to potential counterarguments

(6) The concluding sentence

The essay question:

Using relevant theory (e.g. motivation), discuss the extent to which the principles of scientific management are relevant to organisations in the early 21st century.

The paragraph

*It is necessary to be familiar with the historical context of scientific management theory **(1)**. Merriman (2004) states that at the end of the nineteenth and beginning of the twentieth century the USA was experiencing an immigration boom. Many people left Europe seeking a better life in the United States. They wanted to escape poverty or persecution. However, the life they found in the New World was also a hard one. They 'depended on their labor for survival' (Merriman, 2004, p. 836) **(2)**. Furthermore, according to Merriman (2004) they had 'harsh working conditions' and 'low wages' (p. 837). Many of these people were from poor regions like southern Italy. Many of them were Jews from Eastern Europe. Therefore, they spoke* *poor English, or did not speak it at all (Merriman, 2004). Taylor's scientific management was to be applied to these people, since, as common sense would suggest, they could only carry out simple, unskilled work, and splitting the task into subtasks made it easy to train the workforce **(3)**. However, nowadays the situation is really different **(4)**. Many more people are becoming skilled workers and English is a global language, too. Hence, Taylor's principles are not that relevant. Yet, it should not be forgotten that unskilled labour still exists **(5)**. Therefore, the relevance of Frederick Taylor's scientific management depends on the context in which those principles are applied **(6)**.*

3.3. Creating a Structure and Planning: Brainstorming, Outlining and Mind-Mapping

Why do you need to plan?

There is an old saying: if you fail to plan, you plan to fail. Planning your essay helps you organise your thoughts and makes you more focused. After you've planned your essay, it is so much easier to do your research because you know exactly what you need to search for. Moreover, when you have a plan for your essay, you can show it to your lecturer and they can give you advice about your plan and your essay structure.

Brainstorming

The word 'brainstorming' means generating ideas quickly, without thinking which ideas are better. When you are brainstorming, the best way is to write your topic or the main idea at the top of the page and then write down all related ideas. Please remember that there are no bad or unimportant ideas at this stage. All ideas are good; all ideas are important.

You will select the best ideas from all the ones you have written on that page. However, to select the best ideas you need to have many of them. This is where brainstorming helps: it allows you to generate a lot of ideas without acting as your own censor.

Outlining

Outlining is one of the most common ways to plan essays. When you are writing an outline, you develop your ideas as a list with bullet points. Each major idea looks like a bullet-pointed heading and smaller ideas that support and develop it and provide more information about the idea are the smaller bullets underneath it.

Let us imagine that your essay title is *Evaluate the role of the internet in human resource management, particularly in personnel recruitment*. As you know from the previous chapter, the word *evaluate* means 'assess the value, tell how large or small, important or unimportant something is'.

The outline plan of this essay will look approximately like this:

The Internet is important for staff recruitment

- CVs can be scanned electronically for keywords. This helps the HR department select candidates with relevant skills and experience.

- Candidates can undertake tests online. This helps with short-listing candidates for interviews.
    - personality tests to see if the candidate is the right match to the company
    - skills tests

- situational tests (made of "what would you do if...?" questions)
- **NOTE: Look for articles that talk about this!**

- Interviews can be conducted by Skype.
  - This helps departments save on travel reimbursement costs.
  - It saves money and time, both for the company and for the candidates.
  - **NOTE: Look for some statistics about the money and time saved!**

Mind Maps and Spider Graphs

Another way to come up with an essay plan is to draw a mind map. Mind maps, also known as spider graphs, are very easy to create. First you draw a circle in the middle of the page. Next you write the main idea inside the circle. The circle is the body of your spider.

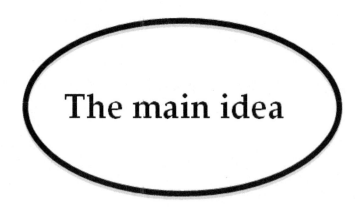

Next, you need to draw a few legs on your spider. The legs are all the smaller ideas connected to the big idea.

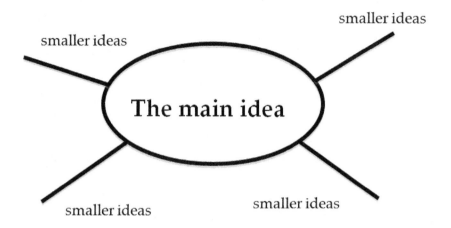

Let me explain this using an example.

Let us imagine that your essay title is *Choose a motivation theory from the field of organisational psychology and discuss how it can be applied to your work experience during your internship in Company ABC.*

You can begin by linking the theory and your experience.

Let's say you chose Herzberg's (1959) Two Factor theory. The main idea of the theory is that employees are motivated by two sets of factors. The Hygienes factor group includes the following factors: status, job security, salary, fringe benefits, work conditions, good pay, paid insurance, and vacations. They are necessary at work. They do not lead to job satisfaction but without them, employees are unmotivated and dissatisfied.

The second group is called Motivators. This group comprises challenging work, recognition for one's achievement, responsibility, opportunity to do something meaningful, involvement in decision making, sense of importance to an organisation. The presence of motivators is not compulsory in the workplace, but if they are present, employees feel much more satisfied with their jobs and are much more motivated to work. An example of a mind map with ideas is provided below.

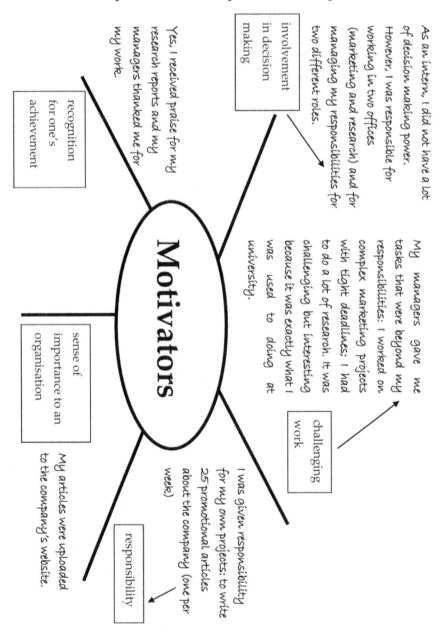

If you develop your spider well enough, each of the legs can become a body and have other, smaller ideas branching out of it.

3.4. The Funnel and the Hourglass. Different Academic Structures

The *funnel principle* (see page 46) implies a movement from broad to narrow. It is mostly used in academic essays with a set topic (see **Chapter 2**). First, you describe the theory that is the focus of your essay in general strokes (usually it is the information you find in general textbooks and lecture slides), then you move on to the application of the theory, for example, referring to previous studies (you can find them in academic journals), and finally you examine these studies with a critical eye (your own view of the theory and its applications in relation to your assignment question).

Reference for Herzberg's theory:

Herzberg, F; Mausner, B; Snyderman, B. (1959). *The Motivation to Work* (2nd ed.). New York: John Wiley.

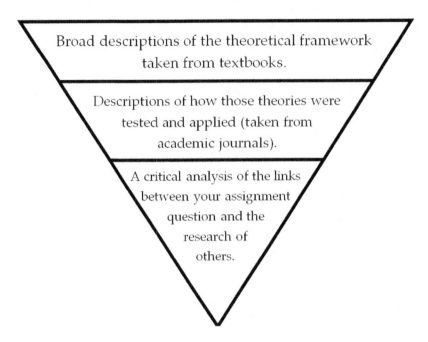

Broad descriptions of the theoretical framework taken from textbooks.

Descriptions of how those theories were tested and applied (taken from academic journals).

A critical analysis of the links between your assignment question and the research of others.

Figure 1: The funnel principle

The *hourglass principle* (page 48) is very different. It usually applies to research assignments with a free topic, where you need to collect certain data and analyse it, such as research reports and dissertations. Your thoughts move from broad to narrow and back to broad again. Moreover, the numbered sections of the hourglass are interlinked.

Section 1 is linked to Section 6 – both discuss theory, but the former gives a broad description of other researchers' theories while the latter focuses on how *your* research has enriched or reinforced the theoretical framework.

Section 2 is linked to Section 5 – both discuss the application of the theory, describing first how it was applied by others, and then how your own findings are related to previous research. Are they similar? Are they different? Why?

Finally, Section 3 is linked to Section 4. You describe your data, methods and experiment design and then what you found post-experiment.

Both the funnel and the hourglass primarily reflect the structure of the main body of the assignment. The largest element of your essay, the main body, is made of a number of parts. There are some differences between academic essays with set topics and research papers/reports and dissertations, where you have to create your own research question. This is explained in the next two sections.

3.5. The Structure of Research Reports and Dissertations (and of the rest of this book)

Research reports and dissertations are structured differently from essays. First of all, they do not have a given topic. Normally, you are expected to come up with your own research question. This changes the entire approach to writing because it adds certain elements that are absent from an essay with a set question – but I will deal with this issue in due course.

Listed below are the elements that comprise a research report or a dissertation and where they are covered in this book:

- **Topic or title** – how to create a simple, manageable topic for your research (This was covered in **<u>Chapter 2</u>**)

- **Introduction** – how to write one and why it's best to write it when you have completed the essay (**<u>Chapter 5</u>**)

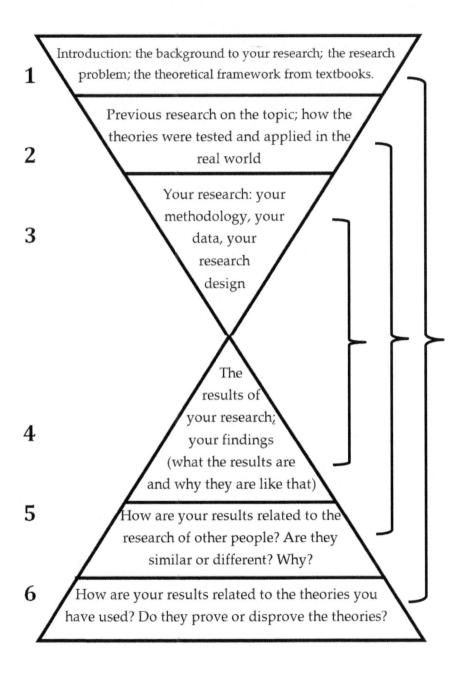

Introduction: the background to your research; the research problem; the theoretical framework from textbooks.

1

Previous research on the topic; how the theories were tested and applied in the real world

2

Your research: your methodology, your data, your research design

3

The results of your research; your findings (what the results are and why they are like that)

4

How are your results related to the research of other people? Are they similar or different? Why?

5

How are your results related to the theories you have used? Do they prove or disprove the theories?

6

- **Literature Review** (also known as 'Previous Research'), why you need one and how to write it (**Chapter 6**)

- **Methodology** – how to collect your data, what research methods you can use and how to use participants in your study (**Chapter 7**)

- **Research** – how you conduct it, what you need to be aware of, quantitative and qualitative research and which research methods are the most appropriate ones (**Chapters 4 and 7**)

- **Analysis and Discussion** – what analysis and discussion mean, how you can be critical about your data, why you need to find weaknesses in your research and how you write about them (**Chapter 8**)

- **Conclusion** – how to write a strong ending and leave a long-lasting impression on your readers (**Chapter 9**)

- **References** – why you need to reference and how to do it, with some useful websites with free resources (**Chapter 10**)

These are the basic elements. However, you also need to take into account certain aspects that are common to all academic assignments.

Chapter 11: What about Exams? deals with exam writing strategies. In many disciplines there are so-called 'essay style' exams, where students literally have to write a coherent essay in response to an exam question within a limited amount of time. **Chapter 11** provides tips for successfully passing these exams.

Chapter 12: The Writing Process explains how to make the writing process smoother, covering techniques such as active reading, writing a paragraph, outlining, and brainstorming. It teaches you how to write more efficiently.

Chapter 13: The Language of Academia explains what the language and style of your essay should be like. It explains how to write formally and academically.

Chapter 14: Writing Tips is a broad discussion of advice on writing. It is made up of two parts:

(1) The Grammarian's Point of View focuses on correct spelling and grammar and lists basic mistakes that you should avoid in your writing.

(2) The Writer's Point of View explains the process of academic writing from a writer's perspective. Writing academic essays is not easy, but the tips in this section will make it easier for you.

Chapter 15: Formatting and Presentation deals with the basic visual elements of an academic assignment. Do you want to know how to present your work in a professional manner? Read this chapter and find out.

So, this is how the book is going to be structured from this point on. And now – let's get down to business.

??? EXERCISES !!!

As we start thinking about the structure (or the 'bones') of an academic assignment, I would like you to spend some time on these activities, just to get you in the right frame of mind:

1. Look at your old or current assignment briefs and essay questions. If you do not have any available at the moment, look some up online (four or five will do). Analyse them carefully. Try to identify the Object, the Context and the Method of the study in the questions.

Please note! Sometimes the context (the *when* and the *where* of the question) may be implied!

2. Download some academic articles related to your subject. Look at their structure. Normally, academic articles have the following components:

a) Title

b) Abstract

c) Introduction

d) Previous research or theoretical background

e) Research question

f) Methodology (the section which tells about the data that the researcher analysed and how they have gone about the analysis)

g) Analysis

h) Discussion (where the researcher talks about the results in more depth)

i) Conclusion

j) References

Look at these components carefully. Examine them in detail to become more familiar with the style and the structure that is typical of academic writing.

3. Read the title, the abstract, the introduction and the conclusion before reading everything else. These four elements are the most important for you – both as a reader and a writer of academic texts. As a writer, you will be able to learn how to structure your assignments and what information to include in these sections. As a reader, you should know that these sections contain almost everything you need to know about any article: the object, the context, and the method of the study, as well as the results. Therefore, if you only read these four sections instead of reading the entire article, you will be able to tell whether the article is relevant for your research. You will also have enough information about the article to summarise it for your literature review (see **Chapter 6** for more information)

4. Read the paragraph below. Find the following elements in it:

a. The topic sentence

b. Arguments in favour of the topic sentence

c. Arguments that present a different point of view.

(1) One of the current factors regarding motivation in the nursing profession is connected with remuneration. (2) Batista, Vieira, Cardoso and Carvalho (2005) have concluded that even though remuneration is a motivational factor at work it is not the main motivator. (3) Other factors have been mentioned by nurses, such as

*stability attained at work and commitment to the population. **(4)** Curiously, when these authors evaluated dissatisfaction, remuneration was indicated as one of the factors of greatest dissatisfaction in nurses' work. **(5)** Nurses considered themselves to be poorly paid, taking into consideration the kind of work that is done, the hour load and responsibility assumed. **(6)** Tavares (2010) concluded that, even though remuneration is a motivational factor at work in general, it isn't for nurses. **(7)** The author indicated other motivational factors such as: liking what one does, an acceptable relationship with the multi-professional team, the possibility of professional growth, the hour load and the working conditions given by the organization. **(8)** Yet, where remuneration is concerned, Vévoda, Ivanová, Nakládalová and Marečková (2011) concluded from a study at 122 hospitals in the Czech Republic that nurses considered wages and the care given to the patients as the most important factors at work.*

Gomes, F. and Proença, T., (2015). *Nurses' Motivation and Satisfaction at Work: an exploratory study at the Centro Hospitalar S. João* (No. 558). Universidade do Porto, Faculdade de Economia do Porto.

Answers:

a. The topic sentence **(1)**

b. Arguments in favour of the topic sentence **(4, 5, 8)**

c. Arguments that present a different point of view **(2, 3, 6, 7)**

It should be noted, though, that the sentences that present a different point of view still do agree with the topic sentence to an extent. For example:

Tavares (2010) concluded that, even though remuneration is a motivational factor at work in general, it isn't for nurses. (7) The author indicated other motivational factors such as: liking what one does, an acceptable relationship with the multi-professional team, the possibility of professional growth, the hour load and the working conditions given by the organization.

The author agrees that money is still important, but nurses find other things more important.

FURTHER READING

Batchelor Institute of Indigenous Tertiary Education (no date). 'Study Skills – Paragraph & Essay Structure'. *Batchelor Institute of Indigenous Tertiary Education* [Online]. Available at http://bit.ly/1oiCsnJ (Accessed May 2016)

Perutz, V. (2010). 'A Helpful Guide to Essay Writing'. *Anglia Ruskin University* [Online]. Available at http://bit.ly/1hbsfaN (Accessed May 2016)

Portsmouth University (no date). 'Basic Essay Structure'. *Portsmouth University* [Online]. Available at http://bit.ly/1qsbkon (Accessed May 2016)

The University of Bradford (no date). 'Traditional Academic Writing'. *The University of Bradford* [Online]. Available at http://bit.ly/1mLY3Ft (Accessed May 2016)

Victoria University of Wellington (no date). 'Structure of an Essay'. *Victoria University of Wellington* [Online]. Available from: http://bit.ly/1hFOfVV (Accessed May 2016)

Chapter 4

Reading before Writing: Doing Research

This short chapter provides an insight into the research process. It will tell you how to conduct your research, where to look for good sources and how to read academic articles in a fast, efficient way.

4.1. Doing Research: Where to Start?

From the researcher's point of view, academic writing is first and foremost looking for the right information, putting the information together, comparing and contrasting different information from different sources, comparing different points of view of different authors, and keeping all your information safe. Therefore, what you should be looking for in your assignment as a researcher is, first and foremost, information.

Now, before we talk about the accuracy and reliability of information (can we believe it?) and the sources of information (who said it? how important is this person? have other people said the same thing?), it is important to know where to look for it. Here are some tips:

1. Start on Wikipedia. Yes, although you cannot use Wikipedia as a reference for your assignment, it's not a bad place to start. Wikipedia is a wonderful online tool for getting general information if you know nothing about the subject, but, unfortunately, it can be edited by anyone and, as a result,

terrible inaccuracies can creep into otherwise brilliant articles. Thus, it is good for getting *general knowledge* on the subject of your research, but then you need to move onto more approved sources.

A good source of information is the list of references that the author of the Wikipedia article used. Yes, those folks also do reference their work. Wikipedia articles have references. Some have a lot of them – dozens, scores, even hundreds. Often their sources are extremely good: academic books, online journal articles, websites of serious organisations, etc. It's worth checking them out.

2. Next, move on to textbooks. Textbooks are valid academic sources, but they have one great disadvantage: they are too general. Sometimes the information you need is concentrated in one chapter and the rest of the book is simply irrelevant. In these cases, you need to read that chapter and go online for more.

3. Use online academic journals. My favourite place to look for them is Google Scholar. Your university also has an electronic library full of academic articles from the journals that your institution subscribes to. There are thousands upon thousands of them in there.

You can also access electronic journals and organisation reports just using Google. You need to use a search code FILETYPE:PDF next to your keywords. Most PDF files are serious publications of some sort.

If you cannot access the journal you are looking for online for free, you can look it up in print. Your university library keeps printed copies of many journals as well. Journals describe specific cases when theories were tested or applied.

4. Then move on to websites as well as online and offline publications of serious organisations (like government or business reports, or even, for example, a blog run by a public figure, etc.) Your sources will also depend on your research question.

5. You can also use email correspondence with someone who has authority in your field of study. This could be an academic, a manager of a company, a politician, or an expert in a certain area.

6. Finally, move on to serious newspaper and magazine articles. Journalists also need to research and acknowledge their sources. A false statement in the press can cost the publisher a lot of money. Naturally, with these sources you have to be critical and take them with a pinch of salt; after all, an article in *The Times* is not equal to an article in *The Daily Fool* tabloid. And even *The Times* journalists' writing should be examined with a critical eye.

Why did I give the tips in this order?

Because the order of writing an assignment is always moving from general to specific. You provide the background and then you move onto the research question. You read the theory and then read how it was tested and applied in the real world.

In addition to these literature-based research tips, here are some general reminders of what you need to do in order to make your research project as professional as you can:

1. Acknowledge your limitations. You need to remember that there's no perfect theory; no dataset is too big; and your participants only represent one particular social group. Your findings are only applicable to your data, not to all the data in the world. A different dataset may give you very different results. You can find more information in **Chapter 8: Analysis and Discussion**.

2. If your research involves human subjects, observe research ethics and do not disclose any sensitive information about your participants (see **Chapter 7: Methodology** for more on the topic).

3. Don't forget to link each section to your research question. Treat all sections as mini-essays; write a short conclusion at the end of each section, explaining *why* what you've written is important and relevant.

4. Make notes while you're reading. Found interesting points in that textbook, chapter or article? Write them down immediately!

5. Keep records of all your references. Names, dates of publication, titles, website URLs, etc. As soon as you get hold of something, note down the full reference (see **Chapter 10: Referencing**). It will be hard to track down later. Keep that list safe.

6. **Back it up.** Your work is your baby. Losing it is painful. Keep several copies: on your computer, on a USB stick, e-mail it to yourself, save it as a PDF because Word documents might become corrupted, etc. If you do not have a PDF converter on your computer, there are many websites online that can convert

your document for free. Open Office also has a free PDF converter and there is a lot of free software available online.

4.2. The Structure of an Academic Article

There is more than one way to write an academic research article. However, most of them are structured in a similar way. I would like to write about it because when you start doing your research, you will find a lot of research papers related to your topic. As a result, you will have a long reading list and it will not be easy to find out quickly which articles are relevant and which are not.

So, let's see how you can read academic articles faster and find out if they are relevant.

Almost all academic journal articles are built in the same way. They contain the following parts:

1. Title

2. Abstract (a brief summary of the article, which talks about the object, the context, the method and, most importantly the results of the study).

3. Introduction

4. Previous research (also known as the Literature Review)

5. Methodology (information about the participants and the research methods)

6. Results, analysis and discussion (the presentation of the results and the discussion why such results were obtained and how they are related to the results of the previous research).

7. Conclusions and recommendations for future research. The conclusion can also contain recommendations for the real

world because business research often aims to solve real-world business problems.

When you start doing your research, you will find many academic articles. It might be difficult to tell what is relevant and what is not. Quite often, not all the parts of the article are relevant. You need to learn to read quickly in order to decide if what you are reading is useful for you.

This is what you need to do:

1. Read the abstract. It contains both the topic of the study and the results.

2. Read the introduction and the conclusion of the article. They contain the key information.

3. Only if you see that the information in these section is relevant and useful, you might want to read the rest of the article, like the methods and the discussion of results.

Chapter 5

The Introduction of your Essay

The introduction is the most important element in your academic essay, research report or dissertation. It's especially important for your reader. Next time you sit down to write your assignment, you must remember that your reader – even if it's your lecturer who gets paid to read your work – is a busy person.

Your reader skims through the first page of your paper and decides whether s/he wants to read on or not. For your lecturer, it is a matter of needing to understand from the first page what you are writing about. Thus, your introduction must be very clear. It must say what the topic of your assignment is.

In general, at each stage of the writing process, but especially when writing the introduction, put yourself in the reader's shoes. Keep asking yourself the following questions: 'Is it clear enough? Will the reader know what I'm talking about? Is it still relevant to the essay question?'

5.1. What Is an Introduction?

In a nutshell, the introduction is a summary of your assignment. It must tell your reader from the beginning what you are writing about, which theories you will explore and what you are trying to prove, disprove or demonstrate. This should be done briefly and should help your readers decide if they want to keep reading or not. Therefore, it must be packed with information, but that information must be *general*. It must be information *about* the assignment, not the assignment itself, and should summarise the content. For this reason, it is good practice to write the introduction when you have completed the essay (see **Section 5.2.** for more information).

Your reader should be able to find out about the topic and aims/goals of the essay from the title and from the first one-two paragraphs (your introduction). For this reason, the introduction of your essay should speak about the topic and the purpose of your essay.

Your introduction must refer to the following:

The background to your study

The first one or two sentences of your essay should provide a background to your study. These should be very general, introductory sentences.

The object of your study

You should tell your reader what the paper is about – and you should do it in detail. Be specific. Be to the point.

The context of your study

This involves not only referring to the physical context of the object of your analysis, but also to the theoretical context. What academic approaches to the subject are known? How are they related to what your assignment is about? For example, if your essay is about the *consequences* of the Great Depression in the USA in the 1930s, then books about its *reasons* will be of little use to you. It is important to acknowledge how the subject was approached by others.

The method of your study

Here you will need one or two sentences describing your method/s of analysis. Once again, even if your method merely involves something as simple as reading literature on the subject and looking for advantages and disadvantages or arguments for and against something, you have to specify that. After all, this is your *method*. It may seem obvious to you as you are the one who is writing the essay, but to your reader, who does not have your knowledge, it will not be that obvious.

Let me explain this using an example below. This is an introduction to a first-year business essay:

Using relevant theory (e.g. motivation), discuss the extent to which the principles of scientific management are relevant to organisations in the early 21st century.

*The concept of scientific management was created by Frederick Winslow Taylor in the late nineteenth century in the USA. This happened as a response to the introduction of laws that protected the employees' rights: limiting the length of working day, prohibiting the use of child labour, etc. **(1)** The employers started to think how the workers' productivity could be increased (Fincham and Rhodes, 2005). Taylor made numerous suggestions, and in his time, they were useful and successful, since the productivity of work had improved. Scientific management was accepted and applied in many organizations of Taylor's time in the USA (Witzel, 2005). **(2)** However, what was applicable a hundred years ago can be irrelevant nowadays, in the twenty-first century. **(3)** Locke (1982) argues that principles of scientific management are still important in modern world, but his claims clash with key motivation theories in modern organisational* *behaviour, as well as the statements made by such authors as Michael West (2004) and Keuning and Opheij (1994).* **(4)** *This essay examines Taylor's ideas and compares them with ideas of other researchers in order to evaluate their relevance to management in today's world.* **(5)**

Here is what the numbers mean:

(1) The author of the essay provides a background, a general introduction to the study. S/he mentions the object of the study, too.

(2) The author continues with the background, providing more detail.

(3) The author presents the main idea of the essay: what was good 100 years ago may not be good nowadays anymore.

(4) The author provides some evidence of both sides of the argument in literature (briefly)

(5) The author of the essay outlines the precise topic and 'says what s/he is going to say'. This is called *guiding the reader*.

5.2. Why Should You Write the Introduction at the End?

Once, when I was working in the learning development centre teaching students essay writing skills, a first year student came up to me and said: 'I can't start my essay. I don't know what to put in the introduction.' What I said in response, was the most bizarre thing in her view, and the most natural in mine.

I said: 'Don't write the introduction now. Write it at the end. Start with the middle part.'

Seems rather strange, doesn't it? The introduction goes at the beginning of the essay, so it should be written before everything else, right?

Wrong.

Unless you are really confident about what your research is all about and are absolutely sure what the outcome of your analysis is going to be, hold off with the introduction.

There are three main reasons why you should do this:

1. Writing the introduction is difficult.

It's time-consuming and you can often end up staring at a blank sheet of paper, unhappy with everything you come up with. Believe me – I've been there and done that. There's nothing more daunting and dispiriting than a blank sheet of paper.

2. You don't have all the information yet.

It's advisable to start *writing* as soon as possible even though you haven't read all the available literature on the subject. You don't have to start the actual essay – instead, you can write some notes on theory, or on research that has been carried out by others. It's good to put something down on paper – just to get the ball rolling. If you haven't started it yet, do so. It will save you a lot of time.

Naturally, you don't have all the information yet. You don't have all your references in order; you've only just finished collecting your data – but it doesn't matter! Just write something. That something can be used later, in the main body of the essay.

3. It is best to write about your most recent activity.

Just finished collecting data? Write about it! Just finished your experiment? Describe it! Just read a great article about someone who's conducted a similar study? Mention it in your Literature Review section. Writing about your most recent action is the easiest thing to do. You've just done it – so simply describe it to get you started while it's still fresh in your mind.

In summary, the best time to write an introduction is when you have finished writing everything else. By that time you'll have gathered your data, conducted your study and read all your research papers and books. In short – you'll be done. Now just write it all down: the background to your research, the topic of your study, what other researchers have done, why your study is important, the methods you have used, the question you were trying to answer and so on.

??? EXERCISES !!!

As you have read in the previous chapter, writing an introduction is not as easy as it seems. As a writer, I know that one of the best ways to learn to write is by reading quality books and journals.

1. Read the introduction below. It was taken from a published article about the difficulties international students experience abroad. Have a look at how it is structured.

(1) International students constitute around 25% of the whole student population (AEI, 2009) and contribute significantly to the financial revenue, academic environment, and sociocultural life of Australian institutions. The sustainability of the education export sector depends largely on the extent to which universities are adequately addressing international students' diverse needs. (2) In recent times, English language development of international students has become a critical issue in Australia. (3) Research indicates that despite the English language entry requirements of universities, international students for whom English is a second language need to develop their English language skills while studying for their degree (O'Loughlin & Murray, 2007; Arkoudis & Starfield, 2007; O'Loughlin & Arkoudis, 2009). Many universities have Language and Academic Support (LAS) programs available to assist international students with their English language skills. However, these programs are offered as a support and sit outside of the main teaching within the discipline (Wingate, 2006; Arkoudis, 2008), with many international students not accessing these services (von Randow, 2005; O'Loughlin & Arkoudis, 2009). This means that subject lecturers are often the

contact point for international students seeking to understand and develop their academic writing skills. Yet, in terms of research, **(4)** *very little is known about how lecturers address the needs of international students.* **(5)** *The aim of this paper is to investigate the strategies lecturers use in order to offer some insights into bridging the gap between language and disciplinary learning and teaching within higher education institutions.*

Source: Arkoudis, S. & Tran, L. (2010). 'Writing Blah, Blah, Blah: Lecturers' Approaches and Challenges in Supporting International Students.' *International Journal of Teaching and Learning in Higher Education* 22 (2), pp. 169 – 178.

Now, have a look at the numbers that I have inserted in the text. Do not read any further for now, just try to guess what the numbers stand for. Why are they inserted in these parts of the text?

Answer: These numbers indicate sections, or transition points, of the introduction.

(1) The introductory sentence. In this sentence, the authors outline the general context of the study and start presenting the reasons why they are conducting it.

(2) In this sentence, the researchers point out the main problem: *English language development of international students has become a critical issue.*

(3) In this part, the authors outline previous research on the subject. This shows very clearly that they have written the introduction at the end, after having read the research papers.

(4) In this sentence, the authors identify a research gap: *very little is known about how lecturers address the needs of international students.*

(5) In this part, the authors say what they are going to do in the article. In other words, they outline the purpose of the study, 'saying what they are going to say'.

2. Another introduction, this time from a business journal, is provided below. Read it and explain the role of the numbered sentences in the text.

Reference:

Voon, M.L., Lo, M.C., Ngui, K.S. and Ayob, N.B. (2011). The influence of leadership styles on employees' job satisfaction in public sector organizations in Malaysia. *International Journal of Business, Management and Social Sciences*, 2(1), pp. 24-32.

(1) Effective leadership and employee job satisfaction are two factors that have been regarded as fundamental for organisational success. (2) A capable leader provides direction for the organisation and lead followers towards achieving desired goals. (3) In similar vein, employees with high job satisfaction are likely to exert more effort in their assigned tasks and pursue organisational interests. (4) An organisation that fosters high employee job satisfaction is also more capable of retaining and attracting employees with the skills that it needs (Mosadegh Rad & Yarmohammadian, 2006). (5) Several studies have also examined the relationship between the two factors and concurred that leadership has significant impacts on job satisfaction and organisational commitment (Lok &

*Crawford, 1999, 2001; William & Hazer, 1986; Mosadegh Rad &
Yarmohammadian, 2006).* **(6)** *High job satisfaction enhances
employees' psychological and physical wellbeing (Ilardi, Leone,
Kansser, & Ryan, 1983) and positively affects employee
performance (Vroom, 1964; Porac, Ferris, & Fedor, 1983).* **(7)**
*According to Mosadegh Rad and Yarmohammadian (2006),
employee job satisfaction refers to the attitude of employees towards
their jobs and the organization which employs them.* **(8)** *The
researchers pointed out that job satisfaction is influenced by many
organisational contextual factors, ranging from salaries, job
autonomy, job security, workplace flexibility, to leadership.* **(9)** *In
particular, leaders within organisations can adopt appropriate
leadership styles to affect employee job satisfaction, commitment
and productivity.*

(10) *Previous studies have examined the relationship between
employee job satisfaction and leadership behaviour in various
settings such as healthcare, military, education and business
organisations (Cook, Wall, Hepworth, & Warr, 1989; Bass, 1990;
Chen & Silversthorne, 2005).* **(11)** *These studies generally indicate
that employee job satisfaction in the public sector is just as
important as it is in the private sector.* **(12)** *Consistent with this,
the present study intends to examine the relationship between
leadership styles and job satisfaction in the public sector.* **(13)** *Two
types of leadership styles are examined, namely, transactional and
transformational leadership.* **(14)** *The specific objectives of the
study are:*

*i. To determine the relationship between aspects of
transactional leadership such as contingent reward, active*

management by exception and passive management by exception with job satisfaction among employees in the public sector.

ii. To examine the relationship between aspects of transformational leadership such as idealized influence, intellectual stimulation, individual consideration and inspirational motivation with job satisfaction among employees in the public sector.

Answers:

(1) Topic sentence that is explained by sentences **(2)**, **(3)** and **(4)**. Sentences **(2)**, **(3)** and **(4)** provide more information for the background of the study. This is a more general background. It also explains why studying this subject is important (good leadership is beneficial for the organisation).

(5) A secondary topic sentence that explains what previous research has found. Sentences **(6)**, **(7)**, **(8)** and **(9)** explain it in more detail, pointing to the links between leadership and job satisfaction. This is a more specific background that is relevant to the topic of the article. This is the OBJECT of the study.

Sentences **(10)** and **(11)** provide the background to the CONTEXT of the study – job satisfaction in the public sector. They also discuss the theoretical context, the context of the previous research.

Finally, sentences **(12)**, **(13)** and **(14)** discuss the objectives, the goals of the research study and the research questions it aims to answer. Note that the topic is narrow: the article is only about public sector, and only in Malaysia. The METHOD of the study is not provided in the introduction – it is outlined in the Methodology section of the article. This is a difference between essays and other forms of academic writing.

FURTHER READING

Note: the resources presented below are not only about writing an introduction. They are general resources about writing essays and dissertations, structuring academic assignments, etc.

Perutz, V. (2010).'A Helpful Guide to Essay Writing!' *Anglia Ruskin University* [Online]. Available at: http://bit.ly/1hbsfaN (Accessed April 2016).

Starkey, L. (2004). *How to Write Great Essays.* New York: Learning Express [Online]. Available at: http://bit.ly/TeLbuw (Accessed April 2016).

The University of Melbourne (no date).'Writing introductions and conclusions for essays. Paragraphs with special requirements.' *The University of Melbourne* [Online]. Available at: http://bit.ly/1kMqHPc (Accessed April 2016).

The University of Reading (no date). 'Writing Your Essay'. *The University of Reading* [Online]. Available at: http://bit.ly/1x8PoiK (Accessed April 2016).

Chapter 6

The Literature Review

When the time comes to write your dissertation (or sometimes even a simple research assignment), your lecturers will tell you that you need to write a literature review. As a rule, most students get confused because they've never heard of this before and naturally the unknown is scary. However, when you take a closer look, the literature review is not that scary at all. Despite the strange name, it is nothing but a critical summary of previous research on the subject. This chapter will make you familiar with this section of your study and show you that everything is simple once you know how to do it.

6.1. What Is a Literature Review?

As the title suggests, the literature review is a review (discussion combined with summary) of all the literature you can find on your topic. The literature you will be reviewing will consist of the following:

- Textbooks that describe the theory related to your topic
- Academic journal articles that describe experiments or studies related to the application of your theory
- Chapters in edited books that are related to your field of study

- Any other information such as numerical or verbal data from various reports, or relevant quotes taken from pieces of serious journalism

In short, your literature review section can also be called 'Previous Research' or 'Theoretical Background'. As simple as that.

6.2. Why Do You Need a Literature Review?

Everyone agrees that a literature review is an indispensable part of every research project, no matter how small. But why do you need one in the first place? There are three main reasons:

1. To show that you have read your books

A literature review demonstrates that you are familiar with the literature on the subject – not only the textbooks and compulsory readings, but also academic journals and conference papers which examine your subject in more detail. You should show that you've read them and are aware of what other researchers have done before you.

2. To show that you know what your own research is about

It's easy to get lost in your own research and start wandering away from your topic, even if you've read **Chapters 2 and 3** and dissected/defined it as clearly as you can. Your literature review is all about getting you back on track. When you discuss previous research, you need to refer back to your own topic. When you make links between what others have done and what you're doing, you remind yourself and your reader what your paper is all about.

This may seem redundant to you. You might ask: 'Why should I write about things that are self-evident?' The answer is because they are only self-evident to *you*. You are writing about it and, as a result, always keeping the bigger picture in mind, but your reader doesn't have that picture.

3. To show that you understand potential strengths and weaknesses of the research carried out by others

Strengths and weaknesses are not objective, but relative to your research – e.g. previous researchers may have used different data and methods. You must demonstrate that you understand how your research differs from theirs.

So, how do you produce an effective literature review? You have to make it *critical*.

6.3. A Critical Literature Review

Your literature review needs special attention. Why? Because it is not just a summary of everything you've read. It's a *critical* summary.

So, how do you make it critical?

A non-critical, 'passable' literature review consists of the following parts:

- The theories you are going to use in your assignment (broad description)

- A summary of papers, chapters, articles, and conference papers that describe how, when and where the theories were applied in the past

- A summary of research methods that other people have used before you

- A brief description of other researchers' experiment design (participants, data used, theories tested, research methods employed)

Now, how do you transform this passable literature review into a first-class one? It needs to involve certain elements:

1. A description of the theory you are using, followed by a *justification* of why you chose to use this theory. You can justify your choice based on several criteria:

- The theory you are focusing on is well-established, has worked for many researchers before you, but overturned some other theory that existed for a long time. You want to reinforce the fact that the new theory works better. Moreover, you want to demonstrate that it works with your data.

- The theory is relatively new, has not been explored much yet and, consequently, there is a research gap that you are hoping to fill. You are also proving once again that it works.

- You are testing a well-established theory using new data. You are trying to find out whether it will still work.

Please note that if at the end of your study you find that something didn't work, do not despair. Try to think why the results were not as impressive as you had thought they would be – and write about it! A failed experiment is still an experiment. It is enough to write that the results are not significant to make a definite conclusion. See **Chapter 8: Analysis and Discussion** for more information on this.

2. A brief description of the studies carried out by other researchers (what you have managed to find in academic journals, book chapters and conference papers), followed by a discussion of how their findings relate to what you expect to discover during the course of your study. This should include the following:

- How your study design is similar to/different from theirs.

- How your dataset is similar to/different from theirs (e.g. maybe they collected their data in one geographical region and you collected yours in a totally different one. Or maybe their data was collected over a long period of time, and you collected your samples within one week, etc.)

- How the number of participants you used is similar to/different from other researchers' studies, or the differences between the participants' sociological profiles (see **Chapter 7: Methodology** for information on participant profiling).

- For example, imagine someone did a study on work-life balance in the general population and they used more participants than you did in a similar study, which used the same process of data collection. Their study should be more representative of the larger population. However, perhaps you used fewer participants but all of them were nurses of Asian origin aged thirty to forty – in this case, your sample would be more focused and representative of that particular social group.

- How your research method is similar to/different from theirs (maybe they chose loosely structured interviews and you used questionnaires. Maybe they used a different statistical formula, etc.) See **Chapter 7** for a more in-depth discussion on research methods.

- How will all of these similarities and differences impact on your results? Will your study have similar outcomes and findings to previous studies? Or will they be different?

Please note that these questions can differ depending on the assignment you are carrying out as well as the subject you are studying.

The main questions that you need to answer are:

What are the similarities and differences between my study and the academic study I am reviewing?

How will my study design influence my results?

The answers are very simple. S/he used A, but I used B. S/he used C and so did I. This allows you to make assumptions about whether the outcomes might be similar or different.

If you fail to produce a critical literature review and simply describe other researchers' work, your lecturer (and subsequent readers) will say: 'So what? Why are you saying this?' It sounds silly, but I will repeat one piece of advice throughout this book:

Don't imagine you're writing an academic paper. Imagine you're writing a Guide for Dummies. Explain to your reader why every little fact you mention is important and how it is relevant to your assignment.

3. An original contribution.

There is another aspect that you need to include in your literature review: your original contribution to the field of study. Of course, at undergraduate level you are not expected to make ground-breaking discoveries. Even Ph.D. students who make significant discoveries during the course of their research are rare. However, it is important to mention the following points, regardless of whether you are an undergraduate or a postgraduate student:

- How do you expect your findings to contribute to the existing theoretical framework (even if it is simply reinforcing the existing theory or 'furnishing clues' to new studies)?

- How are your data and/or method going to enrich the current body of knowledge? This can simply be the fact that no one has used this kind of data or method before.

- Consequently, what is the specific research gap you are hoping to fill?

6.4. The Structure of the Literature Review

As discussed above, your literature review must have the same structure as your entire academic paper: going *from broad to narrow*. Therefore, it follows this principle:

- From textbooks to journals
- From a description of the theory to a discussion of how the theory was applied by others
- From describing how others applied the theory to a description of how *you* will apply it

There is another important aspect of being critical: analysing how the researchers you reference have obtained their data. In your paper you should mention the specifics of their methods because the validity and reliability of a chosen methodology also matters. Please refer to **Chapter 7** for more information.

Compare your study design to those of others. Point out what the other researchers did and whether there are any potential shortcomings in their studies in relation to yours.

6.5. Examples of Good and Bad Literature Reviews

In this section, I will show you some good and bad examples from a typical literature review.

BAD:

Smith (1992) describes a business psychology experiment with twenty participants. The experiment consisted of reward and punishment as incentives for work. A group of ten people were positively reinforced by motivational coaches. The other ten people were constantly humiliated by an actor playing an army sergeant. The experiment showed that reward was more powerful than punishment because the group which was positively reinforced performed the given tasks better.

Why is it bad?

Because it merely describes the experiment without linking it to the current study. Your reader does not understand why you mention this, why it is relevant.

Let's look at the good example.

GOOD:

Smith (1992) describes an experiment that was meant to determine whether reward or punishment was more effective to motivate people to perform tasks. His method included positive reinforcement for one group of ten participants by professional motivational coaches and negative reinforcement (humiliation and punishment) for the other group of ten. During the experiment it was discovered that reward (positive reinforcement) was more effective than punishment. However, there are certain differences between the present study and that by Smith (1992).

In the present study, gaining money for performing well and losing money for performing badly is used as positive and negative reinforcement respectively. According to the study by Jameson (1989) money is not a strong motivator – praise is a stronger one. Nevertheless, the sociological profile of the participants needs to be taken into account. Jameson's study focused on office workers who are middle class employees. The present study focuses on students, and the hypothesis is that money will be important for them as a motivator due to their social status and financial circumstances. However, this does not exclude the influence of praise and verbal positive reinforcement, which will also be taken into account.

(Please note that the researchers' names and the study design are entirely made-up in the example above).

As you can see, in the example above, I am linking the previous research with my own study and this makes me look well-read and immediately tells my readers that I know what I'm talking about. In other words, I know the differences between my study and previous studies. I also know what they have done and exactly what I am doing. This gives me credibility, allowing me to speak more confidently.

??? EXERCISES !!!

Read the extracts from literature reviews below. I have marked some parts of the text with numbers. What are the authors doing in these parts of the text?

The answers are provided after the extracts.

Extract 1

Source: Sawir, E. (2005). 'Language difficulties of international students in Australia: The effects of prior learning experience.' *International Education Journal,* 6 (5), pp. 567-580.

(This extract is not from a business publication. However, most literature reviews and previous research sections are built in the same way, and I thought that it would be useful for my readers to look at different genres and academic fields.)

While generic statements about 'Asian learners' should be treated with caution (1), there is research evidence (2) showing that students schooled in some East Asian and Southeast Asian nations are accustomed to a more passive-receptive style of learning than is the norm in Australian classrooms, especially tertiary classrooms. A study conducted by Hellsten (2002) suggests (3) that international students' passivity is partly (4) due to constraints resulting from their prior learning:

You know in China there are ... lot of vocabulary and I think really good grammar. But ... we can't speak for ourselves. We never tried it. And just, uh ... our education system ... put everything in my brain, not participate. There's only one way. My teacher say. I listen. That's it. So I never say. So I can't speak very well before coming here (cited in Hellsten, 2002, p. 9)

Here the strong focus on grammar and correct usage coincides with a didactic pedagogy, both reinforcing a teacher-centred form of learning in which there is relatively **(5)** *little interest in developing the student as an active speaking agent. Research by Hellsten and Prescott (2004) also investigated factors affecting international students' learning* **(6)**, *and reported on language difficulties experienced by them. The researchers used one-hour semi-structured interviews with first year undergraduate students studying in Australia. They found that feeling inadequate in spoken English hindered many Asian internationals students from participating in classroom discussion. For example:*

It's just hard and difficult. I don't know the feeling, the nuance, I don't know those in English so I ... I am not a good English speaker at all. It's very uncomfortable when I talk with somebody (quoted in Hellsten and Prescott 2004, p. 346)

These studies provide valuable data **(7)**. *However, while they describe the English language problems of international students effectively, they focus on the symptoms rather than the underlying causes* **(8)**. *The research conducted so far has largely focused on language constraints as they have been experienced by international students once embarking on their studies in a new social/academic environment* **(9)**. *One way to inquire more deeply into the problems of international students is to examine the influence of students' prior learning experiences and their beliefs about learning* **(10)**.

Answers

(1) The author is expressing caution about making statements that are too general. She is also using careful language in **(3)**, **(4)** and **(5)**.

(2) In the introductory sentence, the author says what she is going to discuss in this paragraph: she is going to present research evidence. This is called 'guiding the reader'.

(6) The author presents another study which confirms the findings of the previous one. This way she shows that she does not believe the first source she has read; she also demonstrates that she is aware of the existing literature and can compare and contrast different information sources.

(7) The author gives her opinion about the usefulness of the data and justifies her opinion later.

(8) The author critically assesses the benefits and drawbacks of the studies she has outlined.

(9) The author is critically but honestly assessing the scope and the limitations of the previously discussed studies.

(10) The author identifies a research gap and provides potential directions for further research.

Extract 2

Source: Marandi, E. H. & Moghaddas, E J. (no date). Motivation factors of Blue collar workers versus White collar workers in Herzberg's Two Factors theory. *Production and Operations Management Society* [Online]. Available at: https://www.pomsmeetings.org/confpapers/043/043-1565.pdf (Accessed May 2016)

Vlad Mackevic

This is an extract from a conference paper on business. The paper is about the motivation factors of blue and white collar employees. Therefore, this extract from a literature review is about various studies on this topic. The author of the book has retained the original language of the paper but changed certain elements of style.

Armstrong (1971) compared engineers with assemblers (1) using the same type of importance ratings as Friedlander (2), but a somewhat different method of classification. His criteria for work motivation were task activity, the amount of work, the smoothness of work, achievement, promotion, responsibility, verbal recognition, money, the interpersonal context and the physical context. Schneider and Locke (1971) developed a new classification system based on the event agent dichotomy (3). Their study proved the same classes of events produced both job satisfaction and dissatisfaction in both blue collar and white collar employees. These events were mainly what Herzberg et al (1959) called motivator events (4). The results showed that white collar employees placed more importance on task factors and less importance on reward and/or context factors than blue collar employees (Locke, 1973) (5). In several research studies that that were conducted during 1946, 1981 and later in 1986, considering the effect of gender on job satisfaction, a large sample of industrial employees has been studied by Gellerman, Amacom and Aggarwal (6). These researchers divided the respondents into workers and supervisors and asked them to rank ten identified effective factors on motivation. They analyzed this data for gender, job type (collar), income level, age and organizational level. They found out that the responses for male and female workers were not significantly different; however, women placed the factor "full appreciation of work" at the top of the list. They divided the responders into groups by age: under 30, 31-40, 41-50,

90

and over 50 years old. They noticed that there is a significant difference between the ranks of the motivation factors for the workers who are less than 30 years' old and the other age groups. The preferences of the young group, (younger than 30 years old) were good wages, job security, and promotion, because they have not fulfilled their basic needs according to Maslow (1954) (7) as older ages. Unskilled blue collar and white collar workers responses in motivation factors ranking were significantly different. Blue collars selected full appreciation of the work done, interesting work, and good wages as the most important motivation factors while white collars showed interest in interesting work, good working conditions and appreciation of work done.

Answers:

(1) The authors of the paper describe a study conducted by other researchers, which is similar to their own study. This is done so that the results of this study are compared to the results of the previous research.

(2) The authors compare the study by Armstrong (1971) to another study. This is called *critical writing*, when different studies are compared. Comparing different studies is a way to show your reader that you have read widely in your field.

(3) The authors introduce another study. The literature review section usually contains a lot of references.

(4) The authors link the experiment by Schneider and Locke (1971) to a theory by Herzberg. This is also critical writing because it links theory and practice, textbooks to real life.

(5) The authors report the results of Schneider and Locke (1971)

(6) The authors describe another study, this time in more detail. If the study is described in more detail, this could mean that the results of the study are important to the authors of the paper.

(7) The authors make a connection to another theory. They show their reader that they are familiar with the theories, know how they work and can apply them in the real world.

FURTHER READING

The University of Leicester (no date) .'Doing a Literature Review.' *The University of Leicester* [Online]. Available at: http://bit.ly/1xjoKUz (Accessed May 2016)

The University of North Carolina (no date). 'Literature Reviews.' *The University of North Carolina* [Online]. Available at: http://bit.ly/1dIrqO6 (Accessed May 2016)

The University of Ottawa (no date). 'Writing a Literature Review'. *The University of Ottawa* [Online]. Available at: http://bit.ly/1kJ95bC (Accessed May 2016).

The University of Reading (no date). 'Starting a literature review.' *The University of Reading* [Online]. Available at: http://bit.ly/1kGFXlJ (Accessed May 2016)

Chapter 7

Methodology

The methodology section in academic writing normally refers to three components: the data, the participants and the method. The participants are not always present – only if your research involves human subjects. **Section 7.1.** is about **data collection**. **Section 7.2. The Participants** will discuss research ethics and the steps you need to take if you work with people. **Section 7.3. The Method** is dedicated to ways you can analyse your data and describes two research approaches: quantitative and qualitative.

7.1. The Data

Your data is anything you have collected related to your research question. It can be a set of figures that represent the changes in prices over time; it can be a collection of texts you are going to analyse, and it can also be a set of audio recordings that you have collected during a series of interviews.

There are a number of ways you can collect your data. Each one of you reading this book will have a different project to complete and therefore will probably employ a different data collection method. Therefore, the goal of this section is to explain which methods exist and the steps you can take to collect your data from your participants (or any other source, such as the public domain).

Here are some of the most popular data collection methods:

1. Literature research

This involves using both Internet and library sources (public domain texts, social media, online newspaper articles, company reports, etc.). This method is the most obvious one: you read books and journals in order to find the necessary information.

You can use this method to find all kinds of information: you may want to find descriptions of theories and scientific hypotheses, read about how they were tested and/or applied, or simply find out what consumer opinions are about a particular product, service or organisation.

If you read textbooks, journal articles, conference papers, newspaper articles, etc., then it is called Secondary Research. You are not collecting any data yourself: you only read and summarise what others have said about this topic and review the findings of other people. However, for example, if you analyse company reports, interview employees or distribute questionnaires that they need to fill in, or read social media accounts of the companies you are analysing, then you are doing Primary Research – you are collecting the data yourself.

Advantages of Secondary Research

- It is popular and respected in academia.
- It is universally applicable (great for library-based assignments when your research question can be answered by reading books instead of going 'out there' and collecting data).

- It is useful for initial research – finding out the main theories and gaining general knowledge of the subject.

The research methods presented below are all used for Primary Research.

2. Questionnaires and surveys

You create a set of questions, either with a blank space where your respondents will write their answers, or with multiple-choice answers to choose from, and distribute it among your participants.

Advantages

- Multiple copies of the questionnaire can be created and distributed to as many people as you want (for example, the population census is carried out in this way).

- Effective in studies which require a large number of respondents and multiple choice answers are enough – no need to elaborate on the quality of the answers

- Easy to set up (there are great online tools, and many of them are free, such as *KwikSurveys.com*)

3. Interviews

Plain and simple: you ask questions, your respondents answer them and you record their answers in some way in the process (on paper or using a voice recorder).

Advantages

- Participants are free to answer in any way they want.

- Effective in qualitative research where interpretation, not calculation, of responses is important.

4. Observation

You observe your participants and take notes. Also known as **ethnographic research.**

Advantages

- Useful for studying various social groups, children and animals and where observation of social interaction is paramount. Can be used, for example, to analyse organisational culture in companies.

5. A case study

A case study is a detailed examination of *one* phenomenon. This can be an analysis of an event, an organisation, a person, etc.

Advantages

- Narrowly focused, as the object of the study is clearly defined
- Universally applicable across a range of disciplines

6. Conversation analysis

Recording a conversation using an audio recorder, then transcribing it word-for-word and analysing the interaction that is taking place.

Advantages

- Allows in-depth qualitative analysis
- Useful in linguistic, sociological as well as psychological research. Can be used in business research as well where qualitative analysis is required.

7. Measurements

You can measure and calculate literally anything. It can be used in business research to assess, for example, the response rate to customer queries, different costs, etc.

Advantages

- Effective in any type of quantitative research

Naturally, this list is far from exhaustive. There are many possible research methods – not least because the seven mentioned above can be combined and developed. They all depend on your experiment design, i.e. the way you're getting your data.

To sum up, the data is the information that you've collected and compiled in one form or another in order to analyse systematically. Now, if your data is from the public domain (e.g. you have taken a text from an online source, like a discussion forum or a blog, whose author has made it publicly available), you can jump to **Section 7.3. The Method**. However, if, by any chance, humans are involved in your study, you need to read **Section 7.2** first.

7.2. The Participants

Your participants are the people who take part in your study. They don't have to be people you have interviewed personally – they could be people on the internet whose writings you analyse. If it is not an anonymous nickname on an online forum, but a person you know or a person who shares their real name, it is important that you (1) make a social profile of them and (2) observe certain research ethics procedures. Let me explain these two elements.

Profiling the participants

A profile is a description of certain elements that characterise your participants. Those elements are study-specific; in other words, they will depend on what you're trying to demonstrate by your research. However, the examples below will give you a general idea:

- Age
- Gender
- Personality type
- Occupation
- Education (secondary, higher, master's degree, etc.)

The list can go on and on and it's up to you to decide what to include and what to leave out.

See the sample profile below (it is a made-up example for a study on motivation).

Name: Subject 1

Age: 20

Gender: Male

Occupation: Business student

Personality Type: Type A (conscientious, nervous)

Research ethics

There are many reasons why you should carefully observe the research ethics procedures. One of them is because you want to keep your friends. There is an anecdote among academics about a linguist who secretly recorded dinner table conversations whenever her friends came round to visit her. She got some great data out of it, even published a book, but when her friends found out and recognised themselves in the dialogues which she included in the text, they never wanted to be friends with her again.

The lesson is *make your participants aware of what you are doing*. You do this in the following way:

1. Inform your participants of what your study is about. Sometimes this can hamper the results. For example, your participants may be giving you answers that they think you want to hear. However, you do not have to say what you are analysing precisely. You are allowed to be deliberately vague. Be vague if you need to, but don't lie to your participants.

2. Inform your participants how you are collecting the data (observations, questionnaires, interviews, sound and video recordings, etc.)

You simply have to make sure they know. They have a right to that.

3. Do not disclose their names and other sensitive information. When mentioning your participants in your paper, call them *Subject 1, Subject 2*, etc.

4. Tell them that any data you collect from them will be stored safely.

5. Inform them verbally and in writing. Give them an ethics form to sign (see a sample ethics form below).

SAMPLE ETHICS FORM

I am conducting a research project with the aim of determining what effects certain types of leadership have on team performance.

During this research experiment, I will ask the participants to undertake a series of tasks as a team under the leadership of another participant. The performance levels will be measured and post-experiment interviews with the participants will be conducted.

The experiment will be preceded by a short questionnaire to determine the participants' personality types.

The experiment will last for three weeks. Two one-hour sessions per week will take place.

All the information about the participants will be kept safe, secret and confidential. The personal information about the participants' personality types will be published in the research paper following the study. However, the participants will never be named and no sensitive data will ever be disclosed.

The participants can withdraw from the experiment at any time.

I _____ (please type name) agree to the conditions above.

Signature _____ Date _____

7.3. The Research Process and Methods

In this section I will talk about the research process. First, I will write about what research is, then tell you the differences between primary and secondary research, and finally explain the differences between quantitative and qualitative research methods.

What is research?

Generally speaking, research is a process we use to find information that interests us in order to do the following:

- Learn something
- Solve a problem
- Test whether a certain idea is true
- Explore a particular area of study

Research can be divided into categories according to certain criteria. First of all, it can be primary or secondary, according to how the researcher obtains his/her data; secondly, it can be quantitative or qualitative, depending on how the researcher analyses the data. I will explain these differences below.

Primary research

Involves first-hand observations and investigation.

For example, a physicist or chemist experimenting in the lab, a psychologist observing a group of children, or a literature scholar analysing a novel by Charles Dickens are all engaging in primary research because they are working with original data. In business studies, primary research could involve: interviewing company employees or asking them to fill out questionnaires or perform tasks; observing organisations or markets; conducting surveys; reading company reports, and doing everything else that involves working with real business data.

Secondary research

Involves examining and evaluating studies made by other researchers. Secondary research can be carried out through reading textbooks, journals, academic articles as well as pieces of serious journalism.

It must be said that academic research projects often involve both primary and secondary research. However, undergraduate essays mostly involve secondary, or library-based research and research reports, case studies and dissertations involve both.

When it comes to grouping research according to research methods, generally speaking, it is divided into quantitative and qualitative research. The tables below summarises the two.

View on reality:

Quantitative research	Qualitative research
Reality is objective. There can only be one view of the world.	Reality is subjective (it is subject to interpretation). The researcher's view of the world depends on the theory that s/he has employed.

Bias

Quantitative research	Qualitative research
The research is value-free and unbiased.	The research is biased and value-laden.

I must say that this view is also biased. Although quantitative research is supposedly more objective because it deals with hard data and not interpretations, qualitative research can also be objective because qualitative analysis is still done using a rigorous method accepted in the scientific community. Moreover, while quantitative research deals with numbers, the interpretation of what these numbers mean for the wider research context, how they prove or disprove theory, etc. is actually subjective and, in a way, qualitative.

Relationship between the researcher and the object of study

Quantitative research	Qualitative research
The researcher is independent from the object of study.	The researcher interacts with the object of his/her study.

Data examination

Quantitative research	Qualitative research
The data is examined objectively, without engaging in interpretation	Interpretation of data is allowed and encouraged.

Where is it used?

Quantitative research	Qualitative research
It is used predominantly in	It is used predominantly in

natural and life sciences.	humanities and social sciences.

Once again, this is not as clear-cut as it seems. Business research uses both techniques although it is often viewed as a social science.

Research methods

Quantitative research	Qualitative research
Statistics, various experiments, measurements, questionnaires are used.	Text analysis, interpretation, historical analysis, interviews, conversation analysis are used.

6.4. Research-Related Dangers

When devising your research method, you have to be aware of certain research-related dangers. Please bear these in mind:

1. Assimilating with the object of your study

This often happens during ethnographic research – you assimilate with the group and stop noticing its peculiarities, taking it for granted. As a result, your research can lose its perceptive edge. This can happen, for example, if you work in the organisation where you conduct your study.

Moreover, sometimes, instead of describing a certain phenomenon, you become an evaluative journalist. This happens when you get so involved with the study that you start analysing your feelings and reactions to the study as well as giving opinions about it instead of describing it in a detached manner. This is something to be wary of.

2. The 'Microphone Paradox'

I experienced this while conducting my study on the Birmingham accent. I was analysing its features and how it changes over time by recording older and younger speakers and comparing their speech. However, I had a problem: one of the older speakers switched from her regional accent to a more standard form of English from time to time when I recorded her. This could be explained by the fact that the Birmingham accent is somewhat stigmatised, so she wanted to sound more 'standard' and 'proper'. I wanted an authentic recording, but got a fusion of standard and regional.

The 'Microphone Paradox' can even occur without the microphone present. What I mean is that your participants may give you the responses they think you *expect* to hear and, as a result, the data you collect may not be genuine. So, it's extremely important to design your research in a way that allows you to collect the best, most authentic data.

3. Research ethics

Your participants must be aware of everything you're doing and you must have their consent. Talk about research ethics to your lecturer each time your study involves people.

??? EXERCISES !!!

I have taken three extracts from the methodology sections of three published academic articles. In the light of what you have just read, how would you answer the following questions:

1. What do the numbers in Extracts 1 and 3 mark? What information does the author provide to the reader?

2. Why does each author write so much about the participants and their background, as well as about the experiment?

3. Why does the author of Extract 1 use participants of different nationalities and genders? Why do the authors of Extract 3 use participants from different departments?

4. Which research methods did the authors of each article use – qualitative or quantitative? Why do you think so?

5. The authors of Extract 2 have split the methodology section into sub-sections. Why, in your opinion, have the authors done it?

The answers are provided below the extracts.

NOTE: Once again, the first two extracts are about international students learning English abroad. The third one is from a business journal. I have provided extracts from different disciplines for illustration purposes. You could use the methods from Extracts 1 and 2 every time you conduct interviews or even surveys where the respondents are supposed to give more elaborate answers. The same research methods can be used in different academic subjects.

Extract 1:

METHODS

The data reported in this paper were derived from a larger study of English as a Foreign Language (EFL) among international students *(1)*. The study investigated the EFL learners' beliefs about English language learning and how their beliefs were reflected in their communication behaviour. The empirical *(2)* research for that larger study included interviews *(3)* with the EFL learners about their prior English language learning at school. Interviews were conducted with twelve international students *(4)*, from Indonesia (two males and two females), Hong Kong (one male), Thailand (one female), Vietnam (two males and two females) and Japan (one male and one female). These students had just finished schooling in their own countries and had come to Australia to pursue their undergraduate study in an Australian institution. They had been in Australia from six to ten weeks. At the time of the interview, these students were undertaking a bridging program for ten weeks to supplement their International English Language Testing System (IELTS) score as required by the university, a test of the standard of English which is used as one of the requirements for entry into Australian universities. The students were asked *(5)* to comment on various aspects of English language learning, including questions regarding their classroom practices, resources enabling them to use the language in a practical way, and difficulties in language learning. Students were also asked about their language learning experience after arriving in Australia. The interview was transcribed and analysed *(6)*. In order to maintain the truth value of the students' comments, the extracts quoted are presented as they are without any editing. (The number in brackets *identifies each individual participant. Gender and home country are specified).*

Source: Sawir, E. (2005). 'Language difficulties of international students in Australia: The effects of prior learning experience.' *International Education Journal*, 6(5), pp. 567-580.

Extract 2:

3.2. Instrument

In the study, a questionnaire was used to obtain the students' perceptions of difficulty (see Appendix A). A total of 18 Likert-type scale items (5=very difficult; 1=very easy) were used together with four open-ended questions. Among the 18 items, 15 were borrowed from Evans and Green (2007) and three were added for the purpose of investigating students' perceptions of difficulty with writing the method, results, and references sections. These items were organized into two groups: language-related and structure/content-related. All of the 18 items were translated into Japanese by the researchers and then proofread by a Japanese-English bilingual teacher to ensure the accuracy of translation. These items were presented in both English and Japanese in the questionnaire to avoid students' confusion. As the course was taught in English, it was expected that some students would be unfamiliar with the Japanese item key words. The open-ended questions were presented in Japanese. Students were allowed to answer them in either English or Japanese.

3.3. Participants

A total of 95 first-year science students of the University of Tokyo participated in this study. Their ages ranged from 18 to 21 years old. All students were expected to have relatively high reading

110

and writing English ability after passing a highly competitive entrance examination. However, students were assumed to have limited knowledge and skills of academic writing before starting this course. The participants came from six different classes taught by two teachers.

3.4. Procedure

A questionnaire was distributed to students in six classes during the last class of the spring semester 2008. All of the participants completed the questionnaire in class under their teacher's supervision. The data obtained from the questionnaire were analyzed to calculate the mean score of the students' responses to each item. Their responses to the open-ended questions were recorded and their Japanese comments were translated into English by the researchers. These responses were used to supplement the quantitative data.

Source: Lee, N. S. & Tajino, A. (2008). 'Understanding Students' Perceptions of Difficulty with Academic Writing for Teacher Development: A Case Study of the University of Tokyo Writing Program.' *Higher Education Research, Kyoto University,* 14 (京都大学高等教育研究第14号), pp. 1-11 [Online]. Available at: http://bit.ly/1iaCQhb (Accessed May 2015).

Extract 3

Research Design

*Data was collected through survey questionnaires **(1)** from targeted employees working in public sector in Selangor such as Ministry of Domestic Trade and Consumer Affairs, Council of trust for the Indigenous People, National Registration Department, Department of Social Welfare and Department of Immigrations **(2)**. The respondents* *included employees from different levels in the company such as clerical, lower level of management, middle level of management and top level of management (3). A total of 300 questionnaires were distributed to selected public sectors using a convenient sampling method. However, only 200 employees responded to the survey, resulting in a 66.7 percent response rate (4). The measuring instrument for data collection from the employees is in the form of questionnaires which consists of close-ended questions and few open-ended questions and is divided into four sections (5). Section 1 consists of 11 items measuring the personal profile and demographic characteristics of respondents. Section 2, 3 and 4 consist of 42 items measuring superiors' leadership styles and job satisfaction among the employees using a 7-point Likert scale. Data was analysed using SPSS (6). In this study, independent variables are divided into two types of leadership style namely, transactional and transformational leadership style. As for the dependent variable, job satisfaction has been divided into components, which are working condition and work assignment.*

Source: Voon, M.L., Lo, M.C., Ngui, K.S. and Ayob, N.B. (2011). The influence of leadership styles on employees' job satisfaction in public sector organizations in Malaysia. *International Journal of Business, Management and Social Sciences*, 2(1), pp. 24-32.

Answers:

1. The numbers in Extract 1 mark the following: **(1)** the author informs the readers about the origins of the dataset; **(2)** the author tells the readers that the study is empirical (i.e. it involves a study or an experiment in the real world which is used to answer the research question); **(3)** the author informs

the readers about her research methods (interviews); **(4)** the author describes the participants of the study; **(5)** the author describes the course of the interview; **(6)** the author informs the readers about what she did with the interviews.

The numbers in Extract 3 mark the following: **(1)** shows the research method that was used; **(2)** and **(3)** provide information about the participants; **(4)** informs the readers about the size of the sample – this shows how potentially representative the study is; **(5)** describes the questionnaire, including the sentences after number 5; **(6)** talks about the quantitative instruments – the Likert scale (scale from 1 to 7) and the software that was used to analyse the data.

2. Each scientific study must be repeatable. This means that any person should be able to gather the same dataset, conduct the same study using the same research methods and obtain the same results. Therefore, it is each researcher's duty to inform the readers how the study was conducted in as much detail as possible. It also enables the readers to be critical: it allows them to assess if the dataset is representative enough, if there can be any bias in the study, etc.

3. This is done to make the samples more diverse and more representative. The author of Extract 1 analyses international students abroad (in Australia in this case), whereas the authors of Extract 2 analyse Japanese students in Japan only. The authors of Extract 3 focus only on Malaysia. Therefore, they need as much diversity as possible within the sample population for the purposes of their research. However, when you do your research, you do not necessarily need to diversify

your sample: you can use people from the same company, the same age group, etc. if you want your sample to be focused.

4. The author of Extract 1 used only qualitative methods. This is reflected in her choice of method (interviews, which were transcribed and analysed) and in the number of participants (twelve). The authors of Extract 2 used quantitative methods (his research instrument was a survey, which was filled in by 95 participants). However, there are also elements of mixed-methods research – fixed responses to the survey are supplemented by the students' comments and answers to open-ended questions. The authors of Extract 3 also used quantitative methods. They used a survey which was filled in by 200 people, then they measured the results using SPSS (statistical software) and they had an independent variable and a dependent one (job satisfaction that depended on leadership style). All of these techniques are used in quantitative research.

5. There is no single correct answer to this one. However, there can be two reasons: first of all, it looks neater; secondly, since the authors used quantitative methods, their article looks more like a scientific report, and these usually contain a larger number of sections.

FURTHER READING

Education Portal (no date). 'Advantages & Disadvantages of Various Experimental Designs.' *Education-Portal.com* [Online]. Available at: http://bit.ly/SkBvO0 (Accessed May 2016)

Greener, S. (2008). *Business Research Methods.* London: Ventus Publishing [Online]. Available at: http://bit.ly/24V1105 (Accessed May 2016)

Harwell, M. R. (2011). 'Research Design in Qualitative / Quantitative / Mixed Methods.' In Conrad, C. F. & Serlin, R. C. (eds.) *The SAGE Handbook for Research in Education: Pursuing Ideas as the Keystone of Exemplary Inquiry*, 2nd ed. Chapter 10, pp. 147-182 [Online]. Available at: http://www.sagepub.com/upm-data/41165_10.pdf (Accessed May 2016)

MacDonald, S. & Hedlam, N. (2011). *Research Methods Handbook: Introductory guide to research methods for social research.* Manchester: CLES [Online]. Available at: http://bit.ly/1ldmpFg (Accessed May 2016)

Northeastern University (no date). 'Qualitative Research Methods: A Data Collector's Field Guide.' *Northeastern University* [Online]. Available at: http://bit.ly/SkEnKG (Accessed May 2016)

Perner, L. (2013). 'Selected research methods: advantages and disadvantages.' *Consumer Psychologist* [Online]. Available at: http://bit.ly/1qhMybN (Accessed May 2016)

University of Bradford (2007). *Introduction to Research and Research Methods*. Bradford: The University of Bradford [Online]. Available at: http://bit.ly/1OrhcoZ (Accessed May 2016)

Chapter 8

Analysis and Discussion

I decided to combine these two sections of an academic assignment into one chapter. In fact, researchers often choose to combine the two when they write articles because analysis and discussion are closely intertwined. The analysis section is merely a description of your results and findings (*what* happened), whereas the discussion section is where you try to explain the reasons for those results (*why* it happened this way and not the other, making links to your literature review).

8.1. Analysis

This section will be brief. It will describe the essence of your analysis section.

So, what should you include in your analysis?

This is simple: you need to tell your reader what you found when you looked at your data and present it in some way – either as a table, a graph, or some extracts of the text you've been working with.

I cannot tell you much about presenting the data because each of you will be working on a different project with different datasets. What I can tell you, however, is that your analysis, unlike the other parts of your assignment, should be purely descriptive. You should present the data as it stands in the following way:

- In summary, this is what my results are.

- I have some figures that you can see in the graph. If you have a graph, it is a good idea to explain what the numbers in the graph mean, what it shows, in detail.

- I have some responses to the survey that you can see summarised in the table. Explain more about the contents of the table.

Nothing more, nothing less.

The evaluative commentary you are making on your results is called the *Discussion*.

8.2. Discussion

What should the discussion section include?

Your discussion is the section in which you comment upon your experiment, your participants, your data and your results. You also try to explain *why* the results are similar to, or different from, those of other researchers.

Ideally, your discussion should contain the following elements (please note that the examples below are entirely made-up):

1. Explanation of how your findings are related to what other researchers have found

a) The results may vary because of certain similarities and differences between the *participants*. This must include comments on the number of participants and their sociological profiles. An example of this is provided below:

Smith (1993) used only men in his study on competitiveness. Moreover, his participants were all male middle-class office workers. The present study used working-class women and therefore, since the results are different, it is possible that either the social class or gender of the participants could have had an impact.

b) The results may vary because of similarities or differences in the **data you collected and that collected by other researchers, as well as the study design**. The following example illustrates this. This made-up example is a study in which the researchers wanted to test whether the participants would continue performing the task for less money if they considered the task to be meaningful. The researchers asked the participants to assemble LEGO sets, paying them less and less for each set. They had two groups of participants. The first group was told that the sets they assemble will form a part of an exhibition. The sets of the second group were disassembled before their eyes, so they saw their work as meaningless, doing this only for the money.

It has been found that the participants in the first group were able to perform more tasks before the pay became too low for them than the participants of the second group. These findings are in line with Robinson's (1994) study in which he also used a similar study design. However, it must be noted that Robinson's study shows a higher result for the group that had their sets disassembled. One of the reasons could be the fact that his participants received a higher salary for performing the tasks than the participants in this study. Therefore, money can be viewed as an important motivator. Moreover, the social background of the participants might also play a role. Robertson's participants were college students from lower to middle income families. The participants in this study were the students from a private school. Therefore, it could be said that the monetary reward was more important to Robinson's participants than the participants of this study.

c) The results may vary due to similarities and differences in the *methods used*. The following example shows how this is presented:

The results of the present study are different from Johnson's (1989) findings, but he used questionnaires which limit the possibility to expand on the answer. On the other hand, this study used interviews with open-ended ended questions, which allowed the participants to be more reflective and give more elaborate answers.

2. Explanation of why the results are not exactly the same as expected in the hypothesis

The words above are somewhat misleading. Your results do not have to echo your hypothesis – in fact, it is perfectly fine if they do disprove it, or prove it only partially. However, the emphasis here is on the explanation as to *why* the hypothesis could not be proven (or disproved) *perfectly*. By this I mean the need to acknowledge your limitations.

Top four reasons why you should admit your weaknesses

When you're writing an academic assignment – no matter whether it's a first year essay or a Ph.D. thesis, it is very important to acknowledge your limitations.

It is a must for every researcher to recognise the weak points in their work and clearly acknowledge them in their writing, so that the reader would have no doubts about the limitations of the research.

So, where can you find weak points in your academic work? Some areas to look at are listed below:

- Weaknesses of the theory (because no theory is perfect)
- Weaknesses and deficiencies of the data (because your data can only be representative of a small percentage of all the data available in the world)
- Weaknesses of the research methods (because every research method has its limitations)

Here are the top four reasons why you should acknowledge your limitations:

Reason #1: Your lecturer will like it.

Yes, acknowledging your weaknesses and limitations is a sign of a mature researcher and a professional. Doing this will earn you points. Being over-confident and cocky will not.

Reason #2: No theory is perfect.

A perfect one-size-fits-all theory is called reality. It is just as useless as a map with a one-to-one scale.

The benefit of any theory lies in the fact that it depicts a limited view of reality from a single viewpoint, excluding multiple minor factors. It allows the researcher to analyse and generalise, but, of course, the limited view is a drawback at the same time.

However, you have to finish your paper some time, so you can't combine all the theories in the world and write about your topic forever. Just choose a theory, acknowledge its limitations and stick to it.

Reason #3: There is no such thing as perfect data.

No matter how hard you try to make your data maximally representative and useful for your study, there will always be limitations to it.

Your sample will always be too small. The number of respondents to your questionnaire will never represent the entire population. The number of people you interview needs to be reasonably small so you can type up and analyse their responses in the given time-frame.

Even the number of books and journals you have read will not be large enough because you just can't read them all.

This has to be admitted.

Reason #4: There is no perfect research method.

Whatever technique you choose – statistical analysis (quantitative methods) or reading carefully, looking for notable features and comparing what you find against an existing theoretical framework (qualitative research), it is usually one and not the other.

However, if you decide to combine several different methods (which is fine and many people do it), it may mean that one method is not representative enough, or there is a potential for error and you want to re-check something.

In short – make it clear that your research is limited and there is no limit to perfection. Even if your data is brilliant.

After all, research is all about bridging one knowledge gap and creating another.

A conclusion can be drawn from the points mentioned above: your results do not perfectly prove or disprove your hypothesis because your data, method or experiment design will always be imperfect. All you have to do is acknowledge that imperfection.

Once again, I repeat that this is never a problem in academia. In fact, there is a legend in scientific circles about the experiments Thomas Edison carried out during the process of inventing the light bulb. Edison tried ten thousand different materials that he thought would burn inside the bulb, but each time the experiment failed. He was asked by one of his colleagues: 'Aren't you discouraged by failure? You've already failed ten thousand times!' Edison's reply was: 'On the contrary – I've succeeded ten thousand times! I've found ten thousand materials that don't work!'

??? EXERCISES !!!

Read the extract from the discussion section below. I have marked certain parts of the text with numbers. What do these numbers represent? What are the authors doing in the text? Also, pay attention to the words that are in **_bold and underlined_** – these are great examples of cautious language. As you can see, the authors only speak confidently about their findings because they are concrete. When they explain the reasons behind the findings, they are much more cautious and use a lot of 'careful, hesitant language.'

4. Results and discussion

The results of the study show that the students perceived all aspects of academic writing to be difficult (see Table 2) **(1)**. *Since a '5' represents 'very difficult' and '1' represents 'very easy,'* **_it is possible to assume_** *that a score over '3'* **_can be interpreted_** *as difficult. Table 2 shows the mean scores for the items in descending order. As shown in the table, all of the items received scores over '3'.*

[Table 2 was deleted from this extract]

Difficulty levels were categorized into three groups: difficult (points 4 & 5), neutral (point 3), and easy (points 1 & 2) (see Table 3) **(2)**.

[Table 3 was deleted from this extract]

Some **_possible_** *reasons* **(3)** *can be offered for students' perceptions of difficulty with academic writing. First of all, a great number of students* **_may_** **(4)** **_not have realized_** *that academic* *writing is different from general English writing. The majority of Japanese high school writing activities are translation-based and little instruction and practice is given to improve their writing skills (see Kobayashi & Rinnert, 2002) **(5)**. Consequently, they **might have based** their judgments of difficulty on their former experiences with English writing in general. Second, **it is possible to hypothesize** that the students expressed a high degree of difficulty due to their perceptions of low English ability **(6)**. One student made the comment: "Because I am very weak at English, everything was very difficult for me."*

*As shown in Tables 2 & 3 **(7)**, the students expressed a higher perception of difficulty with the language-related components of academic writing rather than the structure/content-related component which agrees with Evens and Green's findings (2007) **(8)**. Items that were claimed to be the most difficult were language-related items, such as item 12 (expressing ideas clearly & logically), item 17 (expressing ideas in correct English), and item 18 (using appropriate academic styles), whereas the easiest items were rather structure/content-related, such as item 7 (writing the results section), item 4 (writing references), and item 6 (writing the method section). It should be noted that some of the items rated as among the most difficult **may appear** to involve structure/content-related components (e.g., writing the discussion and writing the abstract), but they also involve language skills related to summarizing and linking ideas for the entire research paper.*

*These results were supported by students' comments **(9)**. When they were asked which component they should spend more time on, 14 students gave the 'language-related' response while only eight gave the 'structure/content-related' response. One student, for example, stated, "I think more time should be spent on the writing skills. I think it would be better if the teacher could spend more time looking at our* *writing in class." The former, language-related components included students' comments on 'proofreading written assignments'. The students claimed that they perceived 'proofreading written assignments' (item 15) to be more difficult than 'revising written work' (item 3). Proofreading is linked to the language-related components of academic writing because it is a process that involves the correction of grammar, vocabulary, and punctuation, rather than improvement of content and organization by revising written work (Evans & Green, 2007) (10).*

Another interesting finding is with the students' perceptions of difficulty with research design. Student comments included:

"It was difficult to find a suitable topic for our research. It was difficult to find a topic that was interesting, significant, but easily attainable."

"Research planning was the most difficult. I couldn't decide what experiment to do."

"Planning an experiment was more difficult than writing English sentences. It was even more difficult to conduct an appropriate experiment."

"It would have been better if we had been given more materials or examples to help decide our research topics."

*These comments **suggest** that the students needed more guidelines for topic selection. It **seemed** that the research topic design was difficult for these first-year university students because of their limited knowledge and experience with research design.*

Source: Lee, N. S. & Tajino, A. (2008). 'Understanding Students' Perceptions of Difficulty with Academic Writing for

Teacher Development: A Case Study of the University of Tokyo Writing Program.' *Higher Education Research, Kyoto University,* 14 (京都大学高等教育研究第14号), pp. 1-11 [Online]. Available at: http://bit.ly/1iaCQhb (Accessed May 2016).

Answers:

(1), **(2)** and **(7)** – the authors point the readers to the tables, thus referring to the summary of their results and explaining, although it might seem obvious, what these tables contain.

(3), **(4)** and **(6)** – the authors outline possible reasons for their results

(6), **(8)** and **(10)** – the authors refer to previous studies that support their findings. In **(8)**, they explicitly state:

students expressed a higher perception of difficulty with the language-related components of academic writing rather than the structure/content-related component **which agrees with Evens and Green's findings (2007)**

(9) – the authors present additional (qualitative) findings to support their argument based on a quantitative study.

FURTHER READING

Hess, D. R. (2004).'How to Write an Effective Discussion.' *Respiratory Care* 49 (10), pp. 1238 – 1241 [Online]. Available at: http://bit.ly/1hH98pw (Accessed April 2016)

Lerner, N. (no date). *Writing Introductions and Discussions.* [Online]. Available at: http://bit.ly/1uAQEt1 (Accessed April 2016)

San Francisco Edit (no date). 'Fourteen Steps to Writing an Effective Discussion Section.' *San Francisco Edit* [Online]. Available at: http://www.sfedit.net/discussion.pdf (Accessed April 2016)

Chapter 9

The Conclusion of Your Essay

So, you've done it – you've finished your main body and planned how you will summarise it in your introduction. Now you've only got one little bit left – the conclusion. So how do you do it?

This chapter will explain what your conclusion should contain.

As I have already mentioned in this book, all academic and professional writing can be summed up in three parts:

1. Say what you're going to say (the introduction)

2. Say it (the main body)

3. Say what you've just said (the conclusion)

The conclusion is nothing but a summary of your assignment. It should have the following elements:

1. Restate what the essay/research report/dissertation was about. Mention the topic. Draw the reader's attention to the narrow focus of the research question and the data sample (and profiles of your participants where applicable).

2. Briefly describe the methods used, the data which was analysed and, if applicable, who the participants were.

3. Summarise the results.

4. Recount how they correspond to previous research in the subject area. Do they prove it? Disprove it? Remind your reader why your results are the same, similar or different.

5. Remember – only write about *your data* and *your research*. Often inexperienced students tend to jump to conclusions that are full of sweeping generalisations. They tend to say that if something was the case with their data, it is therefore universally applicable and works each time. They tend to judge the entire population by the results of a small sample of participants.

You need to avoid this. Your conclusions should only concern your data and how it fits within the theoretical framework you are using. Do not make assumptions about the world based on your limited analysis.

6. Once again – I cannot emphasise it enough! – acknowledge your limitations. At least say that they exist; there is no need to be specific in the conclusion. You can simply say that more research is needed in order to explore the links between theory and practice further.

In short, describe each section of your assignment in one or two sentences and your conclusion is ready.

Chapter 10

Referencing

This chapter deals with the nitty-gritty of academic writing – referencing. This part of the assignment is something that many students, especially first years, can't stand. I can totally relate to it: you are not allowed to express your own opinion, and even for the basic facts you need to acknowledge who wrote about this and refer to his or her book. It's tedious and annoying!

Yet, this is the way things are in academia. Every thought that is not your own (and at the beginning of your studies this is almost every thought in your essay apart from your own conclusions that you base on other people's research) needs to be referenced.

This chapter will tackle the three most important questions about referencing:

1. What is referencing?
2. Why do we need referencing?
3. Which referencing systems are used in academia?

10.1. What Is Referencing?

Imagine you are talking to your friends and you want to report something a mutual friend said the day before. How do you do it? You say: 'Guess what Michael told me yesterday! He said quitting his old job was the best thing he's ever done in his life.'

Now, this idea is not yours. You may even think that it was foolish of Michael to quit his job. However, you distance yourself from the issue – you mention Michael's name and thus make it clear that the idea is not yours. You are reporting that idea and Michael's words, or you might use your own words to express the idea, but the idea is still not your own. This is how referencing works.

Referencing is a way of presenting someone else's ideas: you indicate the author of the idea, the year s/he expressed it and the publication (book, article, letter, etc.) in which the idea appeared. It is a way of telling the reader that the idea does not belong to you but that you know this information. It is also a way of telling your reader where to find this information if they want to know more about it.

10.2. Why Do We Need Referencing?

So, why do you need to indicate that the idea belongs to someone else – and do it in so much detail, too?

The first reason is simple: because it is fair. It is a way of showing respect to the author who came up with the idea.

You certainly wouldn't be happy if someone stole the essay that you had been labouring on for weeks and handed it in as their own. Perhaps you are so protective of your work that you would be very upset if you saw one sentence in someone else's work that looked similar to something you had written. I can tell you that all academics are like that. They are possessive of their writing and so proud of it that they want to be acknowledged each time someone refers to their ideas – even if only in passing.

The second reason is that failing to reference is an academic offence. If you are caught stealing someone else's thoughts, the consequences may be severe. You will definitely receive a zero mark and will have to redo your assignment; under certain conditions, you may even be expelled (especially if you steal another student's work). You reference because it is better to be safe than sorry.

10.3. Main Referencing Systems

The four largest referencing systems are: Harvard, Oxford (also known as the Footnote system), MHRA and APA.

As I do not know which system your university uses (and often different systems are used in different faculties), I will simply give you web links where you can find them. Please note that the links were correct at the time of publication. More links to different referencing and study guides can be found simply by using Google and there are a lot of apps and sites that can help you put your references together.

The Harvard System

University of New South Wales, Australia:

https://student.unsw.edu.au/harvard-referencing

Anglia Ruskin University:

HTML

http://libweb.anglia.ac.uk/referencing/harvard.htm

PDF

http://libweb.anglia.ac.uk/referencing/files/Harvard_referenci
ng_2015.pdf

University of Leeds

https://library.leeds.ac.uk/skills-referencing-harvard

The Footnote System

University of Hull

http://libguides.hull.ac.uk/ld.php?content_id=4918125

University of New South Wales, Australia:

https://student.unsw.edu.au/footnote-bibliography-or-oxford-referencing-system

The MHRA System

Cardiff University:

http://www.cardiff.ac.uk/insrv/resources/guides/but028.pdf

The Official Modern Humanities Research Association Website:

http://www.mhra.org.uk/

The APA System

Birmingham City University:

http://library.bcu.ac.uk/APA.pdf

Swansea University:

https://blackboard.swan.ac.uk/bbcswebdav/institution/Librar
yISSResources/Referencing%20Guides/Full%20APA%20referenci
ng%20guide.pdf

In addition, the University of Leeds provides a comprehensive guide to less-known reference systems, like Vancouver and OSCOLA:

http://library.leeds.ac.uk/skills-referencing

Chapter 11

What about Exams?

This chapter deals with exam questions. In particular, it explains how to answer essay-style exam questions that are often encountered in the humanities, social sciences, business studies, economics and, a bit less often, in natural and life sciences.

Essay-style exam questions look just like normal assignment questions (see **Chapter 2**). The only difference is that you have the entire term, or at least a few weeks, to write an essay, but only one or two hours to write an exam.

See below for an analysis of the advantages and disadvantages of exams and essays.

ESSAYS

Advantages

1. A lot of time to complete them, plenty of time for reflection and analysis, and you can use spell-check.

2. You are allowed to use books, journals, the Internet and any other resources you need.

3. You know the question in advance.

4. You can give it to someone else to read and get feedback.

5. You can consult your lecturer and your friends during the writing process.

6. Essays can also be written in groups.

Disadvantages

1. Referencing is a pain in the neck.

2. You have to keep backup copies everywhere in case you lose your USB stick or your computer crashes.

3. You have to read much more for an essay than for an exam. Your sources must be many and varied.

4. Let's face it – sometimes it can be hard to get organised as a student because there are ten thousand other things to do and the deadline seems so far. It's easy to wake up one day and realise that the essay is due the day after tomorrow.

EXAMS

Advantages

1. They are quick. Some people are simply better at writing exams than writing essays. There is no need to think and plan for weeks, no need to research the information endlessly. You learn what you need to know, learn a few useful examples to illustrate the theories, write it down in two-three hours and then you can forget about it!

2. No need to reference (usually). Although, if it is an open book exam, you might need to reference.

Disadvantages

1. Time is short. There may not be enough time to proofread or even to finish answering the questions.

2. You might have to carry out your research within a short period of time, keep it all in your head and get it down on paper in, usually, less than an hour per question.

3. You don't know the questions in advance, so either you are revising day and night or trying to guess what will come up and revising only some of the questions. It is possible to guess wrongly. Having said that, your questions are probably related to the lecture materials, so it's not hard to guess what the exam questions will be about.

4. You have to be quick when answering the questions. Almost this entire chapter is dedicated to time management. How do you answer an essay question in a quick and efficient manner, from the introduction to the conclusion, with enough time to proofread your answers? Read on to find out!

Exam writing strategies

The process of writing an exam is very similar to writing an essay. The key elements in this 'race against time' are focus, strategy and timing.

An essay-style exam can be tackled by following these steps:

1. Research.

In an ideal world, your lecturer would give you access to exam questions from previous years. Lecturers are not likely to write a new exam paper every year – instead, it is much more likely that they will only change the questions slightly and add one or two new ones.

If you have access to past exam papers, you will have a chance to prepare some answers in advance. Otherwise, go over the lecture slides and materials. Identify the main topics – those most discussed in class. It is likely that each exam question will correspond to one lecture topic.

After you know, more or less, what the questions will be, you can start researching. Follow the same process you would for an essay. First, read general texts – textbooks as well as the lecture slides. Next, start reading academic journals and more specialised articles. Make a note of those journals – although you do not need to reference anything in exam papers, it might help you gain extra points if you mention specialist studies of the subject area in the exam paper!

Do not try to learn all the topics. You will have to answer two or three questions out of eight to ten possible ones. Focus on four to five topics in depth and revise others if you have time. Select the topics you find most interesting.

2. Practise.

Prepare your answers in advance. Don't try to pull it off on the day of the exam. Look at past papers and practise writing answers to some of the questions in the form of an essay. Time yourself. Keep practising. Practice makes perfect.

Copy your lecture notes – write them out by hand or type them. This will make you more engaged in the process than just reading them.

Prepare draft outlines for your answers. Practise now because you will have to write an outline in the exam, too!

3. Once in the exam hall, read the questions *very* carefully.

They might ask for exactly the same thing as last year, but there can also be a different angle on each of the questions.

4. Determine the order in which you will approach the questions.

This is up to you – you could start with Question 1, or the most difficult one, or the topic you know best.

5. Identify the object, context and method.

Look for the three elements of the question: the object of the study, the context of the study and the method of the study. Then start answering the question.

Just as you would when writing an essay, you need to acknowledge the limitations of your theories and remember that there is always more than one point of view. Provide a balanced argument.

6. Prepare an outline.

As with a normal essay, prepare an outline for your answer to the exam question. Plan the structure and the organisation of your response. This will help you to focus your answer and present your ideas more coherently.

It is also a good time to remember relevant information from your reading and write strong, substantiated arguments rather than just vague statements.

Don't spend too much time on the introduction or the conclusion. What really matters in exams are logical arguments and showing a connection between the pieces of knowledge in the main body.

7. Answer the questions.

Keep to the point. Don't spend too much time on background information. Keep it simple – just focus on the question. Keep in mind the object, the context and the method. The rest is irrelevant.

Don't think for too long about how to phrase things better. Speed is more important than style.

8. Manage your time.

Allow yourself enough time for answering all the questions. It is better to write the outline for each question at the beginning so that it's easier for you to plan your answers later.

Leave some time at the end for revision and proof-reading. Sometimes, when you're in a hurry, mistakes can creep in unnoticed. Contrary to what many students think, grammar, clarity, proper punctuation and correct word choice also count in exams. So, try to make sure that you are writing in correct, formal English.

FURTHER READING

Richman, E. (2003). 'How to Write an Essay under Exam Conditions.' *History Today* [Online]. Available at: http://bit.ly/1xrybRV (Accessed May 2016)

Saint John's University (no date). 'Tips on Writing the Essay-type Examination.' *Saint John's University* [Online]. Available at: http://bit.ly/1jbPsFb (Accessed May 2016)

The University of Manchester (no date). 'In the Exam.' *The University of Manchester* [Online]. Available at: http://bit.ly/1xryIDw (Accessed May 2016)

The University of Melbourne (no date). 'Writing essays in exams.' *The University of Melbourne* [Online]. Available at: http://bit.ly/1oyfzeX (Accessed May 2016)

The University of North Carolina (no date). 'Essay Exams.' *The University of North Carolina* [Online]. Available at: http://bit.ly/1p8U46e (Accessed May 2016)

Chapter 12

The Writing Process

Writing is hard work. Just ask any writer. Even writing this book wasn't easy.

In this chapter, I will share some tips that I used for my assignments at university, as well as while writing this book. I will tell you how to make the writing process much easier.

The key to all writing is *careful planning*. You need to know what will happen paragraph after paragraph. All writers follow this advice – even those writing fiction. If you think that J.K. Rowling wrote all seven Harry Potter books just by winging it, you are seriously mistaken. No successful writer has even written anything merely from inspiration. Every book was planned paragraph by paragraph and chapter by chapter.

You should do the same when writing an academic assignment. Here's how you can do it.

Planning and structuring your assignment

1. Start with the essay question.

Write the question at the top of your sheet and *always* keep it in front of you and in mind. Every sentence of your essay must contribute to the main purpose of your assignment – answering the question.

Vlad Mackevic

2. Brainstorm.

Write down *all* of the possible ideas for the main body of your assignment that come to your mind.

Yes, *all* of them. Later, you will be able to discard those that don't seem good enough.

3. Write an outline.

Write down what will appear in separate sections of your assignment. For example, take a look at the outline of an essay on the benefits and drawbacks of electric cars below.

What are the advantages and disadvantages for the economy and the environment of having only electric cars in the future?

1. Introduction. Electric cars – potential future transport, could be economically beneficial. Research how fast this industry is growing; research the main debates around this issue.

2. Arguments for:

    a. *Fewer emissions, more environmentally-friendly. Research how much CO2 cars are currently emitting globally. Look at the financial side of things. Look at all the costs and benefits.*

    b. *New jobs created in the green economy, new products and services. Find out more about the economic benefit in terms of job creation.*

3. Arguments against:

    a. *Electricity for cars can still be produced in 'unclean' ways – nuclear or coal, oil and gas.*

    b. *People working in the fuel-powered car sector can become jobless. Research the implications for the market.*

c. *Potentially high cost of training and retraining specialists.*

4. Conclusion. Potentially a good idea, but cars alone would not change the environmental situation. A substantial change of the entire system – especially electricity production – is needed.

4. Research your subject

This can be done before you start brainstorming or outlining, but it is better to do it afterwards, when you have some ideas about your topic.

Read all you can find related to your subject and the ideas you came up with during the brainstorming and outlining process. For more information on the research process, see **Chapter 4**.

5. Start writing

Even better – start writing early. The most difficult thing is putting words down on the page.

You have to start doing that immediately. Do a little bit, but every day.

When you are reading a textbook or research article, take notes.

When you think of a link between two facts, write it down immediately.

'Chopping dead wood' off your writing is easy. It's much more difficult to add words, thinking: 'Oh, when will I reach the word count?!'

6. Use transitional words and phrases

These are words like *first of all, secondly, finally, moreover, furthermore, however, nevertheless, yet, also, on the other hand, although, despite the fact that, in conclusion, etc.*

These are the words that will make your writing coherent. Use them well!

7. Write the introduction at the end

It's a good idea to write your essay in the following sequence: *Main Body – Conclusion – Introduction.* See **Chapter 5: The Introduction of Your Essay** for more details.

8. Stick to the rules

Read the requirements for the essay carefully. If it says Harvard referencing system, only use that system. If it says 2,000 words, do not wander from that number by more than ten per cent. If it says 12 point Times New Roman font, use that font.

Play by the rules. These things matter.

Chapter 13

The Language of Academia

Some people say that if you can speak well, you can write well. I would like to agree with this statement, but, unfortunately, in academia it isn't that straightforward. Sometimes academic English can sound like a foreign language – and the ones to blame for this are the academics themselves.

There are several features of academic English that, as a university student, I found annoying – for instance, long, complicated sentences, and 'big words' that authors appear to use to sound intelligent and well-educated. These do nothing but confuse the readers – even if they are native speakers – and send them running for the dictionary. There are also some rules that academics obey out of tradition, for example, impersonal language and the overuse of the passive voice. In this chapter, I will discuss these features and tell you how to write in a style that will earn you points.

Academic writing is governed by a number of rules. Young researchers (particularly undergraduates) fail to follow them and, as a result, reduce their chances of obtaining a higher grade. These rules might seem counter-intuitive to you, but I learned them during my university experience and they worked for me.

So, what is it that makes academic English so particular? There are six main features:

1) Overuse of the passive voice

2) Impersonal language and writing in the third person

3) Big words and long sentences

4) 'Doubtful' language

5) Specific jargon and vocabulary

6) Formal register

Let's analyse them all, one by one.

1. Overuse of the Passive Voice

Journalists often use the passive voice because 'it is the way we do it'; the use of it by novelists and bloggers is frowned upon. So, what should an academic writer do, especially if s/he is only an undergraduate or a master's student and is not yet in the position to write the way s/he wants?

It is true that many academics use the passive voice out of tradition *(the data were analysed; the experiment was conducted).* However, it is not the rule of thumb any more. When I read current academic papers, I see phrases like 'I gathered the data' or 'in this paper, I examine the effects of…'

Nevertheless, to be on the safe side, it is best to consult your lecturer about this.

2. Impersonal Language

For some reason, lecturers do not like seeing the word 'I' in assignments – especially followed by the word 'think'. I understand the latter: your opinion must be backed up by facts. You cannot come to a conclusion without evidence. But what is wrong with using the word 'I' if it is really *you* who has conducted the study?

In the first and, to some extent, the second year of university, you are taught to back up your claims with evidence from the literature. You are taught to take other people's knowledge, summarise it and answer the question that is given to you. Therefore, it is natural that during the initial stages you will have much less freedom and the word 'I' will be rarely seen in your work. However, as you become involved in more and more independent projects, you will be able to use the first person more often, because you will begin to gather and analyse your own data.

Nevertheless, talk to your lecturers for each of the modules and find out what they prefer. Impersonal language *(This essay aims to explore...)* is often used, although it is clear that not the essay but the student aims to explore the subject. In some universities the tradition is to use not 'I' but 'we'.

3. 'Big Words' and Long Sentences

This section is all about 'eschewing obfuscation'. This phrase is a joke among writers; it means 'eliminating ambiguity', or, in plain English, 'making it clear'.

It may seem like the use of long-winded sentences and words that can stretch across Luxembourg is a sign of an educated mind. To me, however, it makes things less clear for the reader. Do you really think that the reader wants to go one paragraph back to make a link between two long sentences? Do you think they will think less of you if they don't have to rush for the nearest dictionary? I really doubt that.

Short words are powerful. You shouldn't ignore long ones altogether, but don't overdo it.

This is the area where you shouldn't blindly copy what academics do. Some of them just like showing off their huge vocabulary. Follow the KISS principle: Keep It Short and Simple. Don't write for your professor. Write for your grandma. Be formal, but do not overuse long words.

4. 'Doubtful' Language

Before I begin analysing this feature, I have to say that doubt is something that academic writing is soaked in. There is no space whatsoever for absolute statements and a know-it-all attitude. The only time you are allowed to speak with certainty is when you present your data and your results as facts. However, you must remember that your data sample has its limitations and you shouldn't make general sweeping statements about the wider world based only on your sample (for more discussion on this subject, see **Chapter 8: Analysis and Discussion**).

In academic writing, being 'doubtful' means the following:

I am certain that some things are the case when it comes to my data, methods and research design. However, there are other data samples, methods and research designs out there, and if I had used them, my study might have worked better, worse or not worked at all.

When you're writing an academic assignment, you cannot have all your arguments in favour of a certain case. At least one argument should be against it in order for you to provide a 'balanced opinion'. Often you are explicitly asked to provide an analysis of the pros and cons or to 'discuss' an issue, which means that you have to give a certain number of arguments proving that something is the case, then say 'on the other hand' and give a number of arguments proving that it is *not* the case.

This 'balanced structure' is the one that academics follow throughout their careers. In general, a good researcher is one who knows the limitations of his/her work and can acknowledge them.

There are certain words and sentence structures that you should include in your academic writing. These are the words that demonstrate your 'awareness of limitations':

- Modal verbs (*can, could, may, might*, etc.)

- Certain adjectives and adverbs expressing a degree of probability (*possible (-ly), probable (-ly), potential (-ly), plausible (-ly)*, etc.)

- Other phrases (*to an extent, to a (certain) degree, somewhat*)

Let's look at an example from a student essay. This is an extract from a research report about the effects of motivation on performing business-related tasks. Two groups of GCSE students were selected for the study. One group was studying a GCSE business module, so they were intrinsically motivated because a business-related task would enhance their experience. The other group comprised students who did not study a GCSE in business but were motivated extrinsically. They were promised an Amazon voucher for participation. The first group would also receive the voucher, but when they were recruited for the study, the experience they would get, and not the monetary reward, was emphasised.

*The results of the present study demonstrate that the participants who were intrinsically motivated performed better during the business-related exercises they were given. They also described the experience as more positive, which **indicates** that they had greater levels of job satisfaction. This **suggests** that intrinsic motivation does have a positive influence on performance – at least **to a certain degree**. Moreover, the results **could be** linked to Herzberg's (1959) Two-Factor theory, which states that personal advancement (work experience for those interested in acquiring it) is more important for motivation and job satisfaction than financial incentives (the voucher). It should be noted, however, that **motivation is not the only factor**, as **some** of the participants from the second group performed better than the average result of the first group. **It is possible that** these participants have a set of skills which would allow them to perform the tasks well.*

Looking at the example above, it's useful to bear in mind two things:

a) You have to speak confidently about your results (in this example, it is the first two sentences).

b) You need to use careful language to express your interpretation of the results (*why* they are like that).

Be aware that individual lecturers may have their own ideas about appropriate academic language. Therefore, it's a good idea to *consult your lecturer* and even ask what style s/he prefers. Keep collaborating with academic staff. Ask your lecturer as much as you can. You will only benefit from it.

(The author thanks the University of New South Wales http://www.unsw.edu.au and Frostburg State University

http://www.frostburg.edu for the materials on their websites that he used to prepare this section.)

5. Formal Register

It is important to understand that the language of your academic assignment is not the language of a text message or a Facebook chat. There are certain features that make the language of academic assignments formal.

No contractions

This book is written in conversational style and I do allow myself some informality – I use contractions (*don't, won't, isn't,* etc.) However, in an academic piece, this is not acceptable. Always use the full form: *do not, is not, they will, it has, it is,* etc.

No slang

It was bare good when Johnson (1995) tore apart Smith's (1989) method and results. That was sick, man, I'm tellin' ya!

Oh, how I would love to read something like that written by one of my students! It would certainly make my day and I would take that student out for lunch – if only to praise his/her originality and richness of vocabulary, as well as to explain the differences between communication in the professional environment and outside of university.

I know that most of you will just laugh and say: 'no one writes like that'. It's true, I am exaggerating. But there are many people who write exactly the way they speak. It is important to understand that written and spoken English are often very different languages.

Use the first person sparingly.

Be careful with the passive voice.

Both features are a matter of perspective and each lecturer might have his or her own opinion regarding them. Do not forget to collaborate with your lecturer if you have any doubts. This has a double benefit: (1) you will get to know each other better and s/he will see that you are interested and will have a higher opinion of you; (2) you will get corrections and feedback, and, consequently, a chance to improve your grades!

Use Standard English. No regionalisms.

In London, it's a *sarnie*; in the Midlands, it's a *bap*; in the North West, it's a *buttie*; in Glasgow, it's a *piece*.

In Standard English, it's a sandwich.

You might not encounter this word very often in academic writing, but you get the idea. As a linguist, I love the English language for its diversity. As an academic writer, I think that we need to have some order.

Keep to the standard in university essays and exam papers.

Also, if you're an international student, you might want to use British or American English. Each has its own vocabulary and spelling system. Please be consistent – use either one or the other!

Oh, yes – and *no* text/chat lingo either!

I wud lyk 2 dscryb de political and ecnmc dvlpmnt of Gr8 Britn...

Ok, I am exaggerating again. But I need to make it clear: do not write anything in shorthand. Your essays reflect your professionalism. Writing an essay is like doing a task at work: if you do it in a messy way, you face the consequences.

I don't want anyone to repeat the mistake of a 13-year-old girl from Scotland who, in 2003, wrote her English essay in text language 'because it's easier than normal English'. The world that George Orwell was describing is not yet entirely upon us and most people would like to keep the English language as it is without switching to Textspeak/Newspeak. Your lecturers are among those people.

Avoid phrasal verbs

Do not *rule out* the possibility of failure – *eliminate* it. Your participants did not *freak out* – they were *agitated*.

The use of phrasal verbs makes your work look like magazine journalism – informal and somewhat slapstick by the standards of academic writing. I have nothing against magazine journalism, but leave it to the magazines. Using overly formal language is not that bad, especially in writing. You may not speak that way, but it will certainly help you if you adopt this form in your academic writing.

Use credible references

This one is related to **Chapter 10: References**. The most important aspect of your reference list is that it should contain credible sources. By *credible* I mean the following:

a) The author should not be someone from the street but a respected professional in their field – either an academic or a practising professional/expert or an organisation.

b) The publication should have been issued by a credible organisation. By this I mean a publishing house, a university or a limited company. It can be published online, e.g. in an electronic journal or on the website of the organisation, but it should not be a private blog or a Wikipedia article. In other words, it cannot be a source that everyone and anyone can edit.

Avoid idioms

When doing your research, you may sometimes find yourself *between the devil and the deep blue sea*. You may be worried that the tasks you will ask your participants to perform might *not be their cup of tea* and that a bad mark for this assignment will *throw your chances of getting a first out the window*.

However, when it comes to putting your thoughts on paper, you should avoid idiomatic expressions. The language should be plainer, stricter and more conservative, even if you are studying creative writing or literature. Your text should sound professional, educated and formal.

6. Explain Acronyms and Abbreviations

I am sure that you know what UNESCO, the RSPCA and NAFTA stand for – especially since you're the one who is writing an essay about them. However, I would like you to explain them to your reader, too!

Never assume your reader knows. Imagine that your lecturer is uneducated and needs everything explained. This is the only way to go about it.

7. Do not make grammar mistakes

Use your spell checker and your head. Revise your work. See **Chapter 14: Writing Tips** for more information on this one.

Chapter 14

Writing Tips

In this chapter, I will give you some simple tips that will make the writing process easier for you. When approaching an academic assignment, each student should have three personalities in himself or herself: the Researcher, the Grammarian (also known as the Editor) and the Writer. I covered the Researcher's point of view in **Chapter 4.** In this chapter, I address the Editor and Writer's points of view, giving some general writing and editing tips.

14.1. The Grammarian's Point of View

I don't like being a grammarian. I don't like teaching people how to spell or punctuate. But I'm thinking about your readers – and so should you.

It is most likely that your reader (in this instance, your lecturer) is someone who uses 'proper English'. Consequently, they can't stand poor English. When you are writing, you should always think about your readers – because you are writing for them. You should aim to give them clearly expressed thoughts, good ideas, logical reasoning – and beautiful, fluent language. Grammatical and spelling errors can be like a slap in the face to them. They will lose you marks.

This is the only reason why this section is important: *to keep your marks intact.*

So, let's begin.

Mistakes that make you look unprofessional

These are the basic grammatical and spelling mistakes that your spell checker might not detect, but your reader will. You should avoid them.

Their/there/they're

The difference between these is the following:

Their = belonging to them (*The children are playing with their toys* – the toys belong to the children.)

There = not here (*Look over there. There are many job opportunities in the city.*)

They're = they are (*Look at the results! They're astonishing!*)

Look at this sentence to see the difference between the three: *They're there with their friends.*

Your/you're

Your = belonging to you (*Congratulations on finishing your studies!*)

You're = you are (*If you keep procrastinating, you're going to fail!*)

Lose/loose

Lose (verb) = opposite of *to find*, to misplace (*You will lose marks if you do not obey essay writing rules!*)

Loose (adjective) = not tight (*Those clothes are quite loose.*)

164

Quiet/quite

Quiet (adjective) = not loud, silent (*You are being very quiet today. Is anything the matter?*)

Quite (adverb) = rather (*The data set is quite small.*)

No/know

No = opposite of yes (*There is no proof that your theory is correct.*)

Know (verb) = to be aware of; to have knowledge of (*I know that the experiment will be successful – I've done it before.*)

It's/its

Its = belonging to it (*The questionnaire has its limits.*)

It's = it is (*It's obvious that the data set is not large enough.*)

Would of/would have

This is another common error. The best way to avoid it is to think what this verbal construction is made of. It is made of the modal verb *would* + a verb in the Present Perfect tense (*have been, have done*). Since you would not normally write ~~I of been~~ or ~~you of done~~, the construction is always *would have done, could have been, should have analysed.*

Whose/who's

Whose is a pronoun. It means *belonging to someone*. (*Whose book is it?*)

Who's is the short form of *who is* or *who has.* (**Who's** *responsible for collecting the questionnaires after the study?* **Who's** *conducted this kind of study before?*)

Less/fewer

Less is used with uncountable nouns, like milk, bread, energy or money. (*Due to budget cuts,* **less money** *was spent on research and development in the company this year than last year*)

Fewer is used with countable nouns like light bulbs, ideas, participants, etc. (*Jones (2005) used* **fewer participants** *in his study than Adams (2003) did.*)

Effect/affect

Effect is a noun. It means *impact.* (*This study will examine* **the effect** *of globalisation on business practices in Poland.*)

Affect is a verb. To affect = to have an effect (*The aim of this essay is to examine how social media marketing* **affects** *consumers' propensity to buy.*)

Then/than

Then is used for time and sequence. Then = not now, later (*The data were summarised and* **then** *exported into the table.*)

Than is used for comparison. (*The number of participants was lower* **than** *was expected.*)

The apostrophe rules

This is my personal pet peeve and a topic that has been discussed many times before. But, as a writer, and as an involuntary grammarian, I must remind my readers of these simple rules:

The apostrophe is used in many situations; however, the two most common rules are the following ones: when we identify the owner and when we shorten words. It is not used for plurals.

The owner rule

When there is only one owner whose name ends in 's', you place an apostrophe and another 's' after it.

The pencil belongs to James, so it is *James's pencil.*

If there is more than one owner and the plural ends in 's', you just place an apostrophe after that final 's'.

For instance, if the house belongs to the Smith family, it is *the Smiths' house.*

If the name of the owner ends in another letter, then you put an apostrophe and an 's'.

For example, if a car belongs to John it's *John's car.*

The same applies if the owner is in the plural and the plural ends in another letter:

Men's toilets – because the toilets are for men and thus 'belong to them'.

The shortening rule

This one is even simpler. When words are shortened, the apostrophe takes the place of the missing letter(s).

Do not = don't

Cannot = can't

Will not = won't

You are = you're

They are = they're

Would not = wouldn't

I have = I've

She is = she's

It is or it has = it's

Who is or *who has = who's*

14.2. The Writer's Point of View

As a writer, I must remind my readers that the process of writing is inevitably linked to the process of rewriting. As I have said before, writing is hard work. This section explains what this phrase really means:

1. There is no such thing as a perfect first draft. You will have to rewrite your essays, research reports and dissertations.

So, you will have to get good at *rewriting*!

2. Do not rewrite or edit anything before you complete the first draft. Yes, I mean it. Do not edit anything. When you open the unfinished document, start from where you stopped last time. Otherwise you might perfect your first paragraph or chapter but never write the second one.

3. After you finish your first draft, let it lie for a day or two. If you have no time and the deadline is fast approaching, leave if for several hours and go and do something else. Then come back to it and look at it with fresh eyes.

4. It's OK to get sick and tired of writing. Take a break.

5. Don't spend all day at the computer or working on a sheet of paper. Write in bursts of 30 minutes and then do something else for five minutes (ideally a physical task). However, if you feel like writing for a longer period, you're welcome to do it. Everybody is different.

6. Never leave the sheet of paper blank. Write something. Brainstorm, write whatever ideas on the topic come to mind, set out a basic structure, or think what kind of arguments your work might contain. Do anything, just please don't leave a blank sheet.

7. The hardest thing is starting.

8. The next hardest thing is doing what you started for the first five minutes without getting distracted. Keep doing it – after five minutes it will become easier.

9. Persevere. Writing is not an easy task. I am trying to help you by writing this book, but I can't write your work for you. You have to push yourself a little. Just write and see those letters connect and form words, words form sentences, sentences form paragraphs, etc.

10. Good writers also read. Read as much as you can – books, academic papers, newspaper articles and anything you can find related to your subject. Read to boost your vocabulary; read to see how academic papers are structured and in what style they are written; read to enhance your knowledge. Reading does pay off.

11. Carry a notebook everywhere. You never know when and where a great idea might strike you.

12. Do not try too hard to write like an academic. By all means, use a thesaurus in order not to repeat a word, but refrain

from overusing 'big words' and long sentences. Being clear pays off much more. Imagine that your grandma will be reading this. Write it in a way she would understand. Do not be informal, just be clear.

I got my First-Class degree with my grandma in mind.

13. Writers write, that's what they do. But they also go for walks, work out in the gym and visit the swimming pool. Don't forget about physical activity – it will help you unwind and relax. It also stimulates creativity.

14. Have fun and keep writing!

Chapter 15

Formatting and Presentation

Flip the pages back and look at this book. Do not *read* it, just *look* at it. Look at how the chapter names are placed in the centre of the page, how the paragraphs are indented, how the margins are of the same size on every page and how the text is justified on both sides.

This is called *formatting*.

This element of your academic writing is just as important as anything I've mentioned previously. Why? Because your work must look professional. You also get marks for it. It is worth about 5 per cent, which could be the difference between a 2:1 and a first-class degree. The purpose of formatting is not only to make your work look pretty. It's also to make it easy to read. Remember, when you write something, always think about your reader.

So, how do you format your work? There are many ways and guidelines differ from university to university (sometimes even from lecturer to lecturer), but there are some general rules to follow:

1. Uniform fonts

Sometimes the computer is set by default to one particular font which you don't really like. Make sure that it doesn't

Vlad Mackevic

accidentally jump to that font when you hit the Enter key or the Arrow Down key.

2. No fancy fonts

Plain, simple ones like Times or Arial are the best ones. You can also use Tahoma, Garamond or Palatino Linotype. Don't experiment – unusual fonts are not professional and can be difficult to read. Font size should normally be between 12 and 14 points.

3. At least one-inch margins

Even better to leave 3 cm (1.25 inch). Your lecturers will be making comments in the margins, so leave them plenty of space. If you intend to bind your work, leave additional space, about 1 cm or ½ inch on the left-hand side (the Gutter in Page Setup settings in Word).

4. At least 1.5 point line spacing. Double spacing is even better.

Once again, make it easy to read. Have mercy on your lecturer's eyes. He/she will have to read dozens if not hundreds of papers.

5. Page numbers

Even if your work is stapled firmly, after being handled by many pairs of hands it can come apart. Do not make your lecturer suffer, trying to figure out which page comes after which. The best page number format is *Page X of Y*. For example, *Page 1 of 15*, *Page 2 of 15*, etc.

6. Sections

If your work is longer than 2000 words, it is advisable to divide it into sections. In fact, you can add sections to an assignment of any length – just name them 'Introduction', 'Arguments for', 'Arguments against', 'Discussion', 'Conclusion', or according to whatever they contain. This will make it easier for your reader to navigate your work.

Read some academic papers to see how they are structured and follow that structure.

7. A table of contents

Add a table of contents, listing all the sections with the page numbers (especially if your work is longer than ten pages, or 2000 words). Guide your reader – especially if that reader is your lecturer who has sixty (or sometimes 600) other essays to read for this module and, to be honest, is quite tired of reading them.

8. The cover page

Add a simple cover page with your student number, the module code and the title of the work (requirements may differ from subject to subject). Your university should have guidelines – refer to them or ask your lecturer to find out which specific formatting rules you need to follow.

Conclusion

So, you've reached the end of this book. I hope I've taught you something useful and reminded you of some of the things you already know.

So, what is the next step?

Apply all you've learnt. First, have a look at your old assignments. Do they contain the elements they should contain? Is everything you say somehow related to the title of the assignment? Do you make explicit links between the sections? Do you go from general to specific?

Now think about the assignment you have to do and make sure everything you write is coherent, relevant and correct.

Start right now.

Plot it. Brainstorm. Make notes while you're reading. Plan the sections of your assignment. What will they contain? How will they be structured? If in doubt, refer back to this book.

Oh yes – and one more thing. Be a real academic. Don't just believe what I write. Check other sources. Talk to your lecturer. Read other books and websites.

Write your killer essay! Get that First-Class degree!

Have fun and keep writing!

Vlad Mackevic.

About the Author

VLAD MACKEVIC is an author entrepreneur and an academic writing consultant. He holds a first-class degree in International Relations and English Language from Aston University, an MA in Translation from the University of Bristol and is currently studying a PhD in Applied Linguistics. During his professional life, he has worked in a number of teaching and administrative roles. This book was written to sum up Vlad's professional and academic knowledge and to share it with you for your benefit and enjoyment.

Connect to Vlad online:

The Lecture Room

www.TheLectureRoom.co.uk

http://vladmackevic.wordpress.com

Facebook

https://www.facebook.com/thelectureroom1

LinkedIn

http://www.linkedin.com/in/vladmackevic

Space for Your Notes

Space for Your Notes

Space for Your Notes

Space for Your Notes

Printed in Great Britain
by Amazon

59105066R00108